PRAISE FOR
RAISED BY WC

"In this utterly original conversation o
Amang and Steve Bradbury offer literary ᵣ
accomplished graphic displays of what it actually means to tra...
poem. Or thirty-two. It is a serious lesson on craft, and an incredibly
engaging record of the processes that two bright, persistent, and
original minds enter into in the effort to create a series of entirely
new metaphors in the world, which are essentially how poems
in translation manifest themselves. Raised by Wolves is
a captivating read and a wonderfully inventive and energetic
contribution to the necessary dialogue about literary translation that
needs continually to be re-imagined."

—Sidney Wade, author of
Deep Gossip: New and Selected Poems

"Raised by Wolves makes one wonder if a wolf cub wrote
these lines, aided by well-tuned ears and able hands. The sensual, nim-
ble and elastic shakes and bounces of Amang's poetry are rendered
into English by Bradbury without losing their alluring presence. 'Get
trashy,' 'to ignore all the rules about how we should act,' and 'to laugh
in their face,' as Amang puts it in one of her lively conversations with
her translator, which are delightfully included in the collection, all are
a form of resistance. Perhaps we need to heed this she-wolf's voice as,
with her echoing howls, she braves the traps of Chinese poetic and
social traditions."

—Zhang Er, author of
First Mountain

"I loved moving through this book, which comes at such an
important moment, offering a much-needed buoyancy to an
otherwise difficult time. Amang's poems, so lovingly and knottily
languaged in Chinese, are the headwaters of Steve Bradbury's fluid
translations. Yet translations, like rivers themselves, are not linear
channels connecting point A to point B, but are continually fed

by a far larger network of intermingling tributaries all along the way. Books of poetry in translation rarely make room for, let alone chart, the wandering, braided, and sinuous transformations a work goes through in its passage from one language to another, yet thanks to the inclusion of transcriptions of the translator's conversations with the author, readers can experience that process for themselves. `Raised by Wolves` is a wonder to behold."

—Jonathan Stalling, author of
Lost Wax: Translation through the Void.

"Deftly translated into a luscious echolalia, these deliciously gritty poems are dangerously charged, like a birthday cake kiss laden with horseshit and broken glass, whispered intimacies exploding into ruined runes."

—Rob Wilson, author of
Be Always Converting, Be Always Converted: an American Poetics

"When I agreed to review `Raised by Wolves`, I thought I had signed up to read a translation of contemporary Taiwanese poetry. I very quickly realized my mistake: `Raised by Wolves` is much more than that; it is an invitation to partake in a feast of words that agree to disagree, that clash and dissolve to reemerge in another language. It is also an act of transgressive eavesdropping, as the poet and her translator let readers in on their intimate discussions about their craft (the book's subtitle is 'poems and conversations')."

— Filip Noubel, *Asymptote Journal*

raised by wolves

poems and conversations

amang

translated by
steve bradbury

PHONEME
MEDIA

DEEP
VELLUM

DALLAS, TEXAS

Phoneme Media, an imprint of Deep Vellum
3000 Commerce St., Dallas, Texas 75226
deepvellum.org · @deepvellum

Deep Vellum is a 501c3 nonprofit literary arts organization
founded in 2013 with the mission to bring
the world into conversation through literature.

ISBN: 978-1-944700-91-1 (paperback) | 978-1-64605-020-8 (ebook)
Library of Congress Control Number: 2020940567

Distributed by Consortium Book Sales & Distribution

Cover design by Justin Childress | justinchildress.co
Cover photograph by Amang

Interior by Kirby Gann

Printed in the United States of America

CONTENTS

THE COVE PARK/MELROSE TRANSLATIONS

TRANSLATOR'S PREFACE

This book has had an unusually prolonged gestation. It began in 2014 when our editor and publisher, David Shook, who had chanced upon a few of my Amang translations online, wrote the poet to ask if she would be amenable to his publishing a book-length collection of her work in English translation. It was a bold gesture given the meager sampling he had seen, and, to this day, I am not quite sure if David was moved by the quality of my translations or by the photos I had posted of Amang's first book, *ON/ OFF*, which the poet, with her customary penchant for making an impression, had had bound in brown sandpaper. In any case, it is clear to me that it was clear to David that if a book did result from his invitation, it would be off the beaten path.

Amang and I were thrilled at the prospect of being published by Phoneme Media, but I had only completed seven translations at the time of the invitation and had just given notice to my employer that I was leaving Taiwan and returning to my native Florida to pursue art. Although I managed to finish a few more translations before I left, I was soon swept up by my new life and did not get back to the book until nearly two years later, when, thanks to a generous grant from the Henry Luce Foundation, Amang and I were invited to spend what proved to be four wonderfully productive weeks at the Vermont Studio Center (VSC) in the tiny little town of Johnson, Vermont.

Like other poets I translate, Amang is very fond of language games, and her poetry is consequently filled with puns, squirrelly rhymes, and other forms of language play that are often difficult to render into English without a significant degree of loss or gain. Being able to sit down with the poet to discuss options for representing challenging passages made all the difference in the world between a polished translation and a poor excuse for one. We did this after lunch nearly every day at Journey's End, a stream-fed, cascade-filled hemlock forest about a forty-minute walk up the road from the VSC. It was our practice to bring wine and cheese and fresh-baked bread with us and to work until the late afternoon, when we would walk back down to the VSC for dinner. It was early fall, an idyllic setting in which to work, and our conversations were so lively and engaging, and touched on so many topics relating to poetry and translation, that I began recording them on my smart phone with a view to including a few in our book.

Too often poetry in translation is presented as if a translation were a mirror image of its source text and the source text itself as clear as glass. But as our conversations, which we continued two years later when Amang was invited for a monthlong residency in Scotland, will show, the translation of poetry is at best a messy business, especially between languages as far apart— indeed, a world apart—as Chinese and English. But what also prompted me to record our conversations was the thought that if readers liked Amang's poetry they would be curious to know something about her. And I don't just mean the dry facts one finds in a contributor's bio. I wanted readers to get to know this extraordinary woman as I have, to get a glimpse of what makes her tick, what drives her to write, what distinguishes her from all those around her.

Before closing, I would like to thank the many artists and writers we met during our stay in Vermont, many of whom were personally inspiring or provided constructive advice during the craft talks that were held every week or over dinner in the lounge. We would also like to thank Will Evans and his designer for allowing us to include so many of our drawings and photos. Last but not least, a special thanks to Lisa Rose Bradford, who read every translation in this book and suggested many an improvement thereto.

Steve Bradbury, Melrose, Florida

Not Yet

有一個吻
還沒到
半路彎腰撿拾掉落的包袱
裙裾上
碎玻璃及馬糞
小甲蟲的春天
體液橫流
橫著流
魚戲蓮葉
　　　　　不辨方向
　　　　　影響力
　　　　　不辨方向
　　　　　頸上之指印
之不易維持
　　　　　不辨方向
但所有柳樹又發了芽
或許他為
乘馬南來展覽著
　　　　　　　江南風景
那麼個角色
天地皆黑　　　我
兩手垂下　　　不承認
那也是
我
最愛乘坐的木馬

Not Yet

There is a kiss
which still in transit
stoops to gather up its bundle of effects
the skirt caked with
horseshit and slivers of broken glass
the juices
of a beetled spring
flooding
carp frolic among the lotus leaves
      this way and that
      allurement
      this way and that
      prints on a clavicle
slipping through your fingers
      this way and that
willow buds are bursting
or else it's just a pageant staged by
this man on horseback approaching
      our luscious southern clime
O these dark and silent types . . .
the light fails
my hands fall   and I refuse to say
yes this is
my
favorite carousel as well

愛情真美麗

她不情願但她
爬下梯子說
愛

如此說令嘴巴歡喜而
對面的嘴巴喜歡
可以
接吻了：
用一根鐵絲靈巧地侵入
搬弄生動細小的鎖孔。可以

偷了

0變成∞, 雖然很遠

雖然她不情願
她仍然用它鑽洞, 用它
埋下地雷

如此做令手讚歎而
對面的手感激
可以
擁抱了：
四條蛇, 扭曲起來
到空中洗澡

泡在浴缸把0吹成∞, 吹出：
穩重
均衡
可以
非常能

Love Is Ever So Lovely

She is loath to but still she comes
down the ladder saying
love

Saying this pleases her lips
and other lips are pleased as well
smoothing the progress of a
kiss:
a bit of wire deftly wormed into a
small but lively keyhole. Which in turn leaves the door ajar

for a break-in

0 becomes ∞, and even though there's still a distance

even though she's not yet fully willing, still
she uses it to hollow out a hole, to lay, as it were, a land-
mine

Doing this she pleases her hands
and other hands are grateful
which thus enables an
embrace:
doubled pairs of coupling serpents coiling up
as if to bathe in the air

Sharing this bath, they blow a 0 into ∞
steadily
evenly
and so
double

雙倍承受的

樣子
很好看

their capacity to bear this
display
so pleasing to the eye

這一首

很淺很淺
你可以進來玩水
不想弄濕衣服把褲腳捲起來就可以
我們可以一起找蝦
翻開石頭
看魚
再打打水漂~~~
從前有莊周和惠子辯論
現在有泳池裡的讀書會
討論「魚式游泳」
還有水中攝影機追蹤攝影矯正泳姿
不過我覺得獵人最厲害
他丟了一塊石頭
瞄準魚洞
水波的力道把魚震昏
我也希望有那一手
特別是更好的還在後頭
20分鐘後
魚
又活了

This Poem

is shallow
but you can splash your feet around in it
if you don't want your trousers getting wet, then roll them up
we can look for shrimp
among the rocks
watch the fish
we can skip one stone after another
Zhuangzi and Huizi once debated
whether fish were happy when they swam
nowadays public swimming pools hold classes
to teach you how to "swim like a fish"
can even video your stroke to help you improve it
but no one can hold a candle to the aborigine
who can drop a stone into a watery lair
and stun a fish
how I wish I had this gift
the best part of which was seeing
that fish
some twenty minutes later
returning to life

多一個

多一個:
不能裝下
秘密的撲滿
多一個:
使今天超出它的體重
多一個:
我溢出
我
不再是「我吃飯」、
「我走路」、「我睡覺」
你認識的我——瓶裡的我——
是假的
她說的話不要相信
如骨包骨, 肉包肉
重瓣的, 重瓣的玫瑰
令花園狹窄, 蜜蜂彎曲
我將辛苦——哦, 不是我——
懷胎
二十小時
二十個月
二十年
但什麼也不生下來
沒有雨
沒有雨
天空佈滿積雲、鐵砧
僅僅是多一個
多一個
多一個
陰險的胎兒
它寄生
蜷曲在子宮裡的子宮

More than One

More than one
is more than
my piggy bank of secrets can hold
more than one
is more weight than this day can bear
more than one:
I'm brimming
with mes
no more the "I'm eating"
"I'm walking," "I'm sleeping"
the me you know—the me in the jar—
is a sham
so don't believe a word she says
bones within bones, flesh enfleshed
heavy-petaled, double-petaled roses

leave the garden too confining, the bees weaving
what a labor this will be—O, not me!
heavy with child
a score of hours
score of months
score of years
nothing ever born from this
not a single drop of rain
not a single drop
though the sky is filled with towering nimbi, anvils
by merely being more than one
more than one
more than one
wily fetus
living off other lives
curled inside the womb of the womb

Error 400 — 418

我想你
400 Bad Request

我好想你
403 Forbidden

我非常想你
402 Payment Required

我要見你
404 Not Found 網頁不存在

(所用伺服器無法顯示網頁, 最有可能原因:
您並未連線至網際網路、該網站發生問題、您輸入的位址錯
    誤)

我只是想見見你嘛
415 Unsupported Media Type

我一定要見到你!
426 Upgrade Required

咬你喔。。。
423 Locked

瞎覓?!把你封鎖
405 Method Not Allowed

最討厭你
451 Redirect 重新導向

Error 400 – 418

I miss you
400 Bad Request

I want you
403 Forbidden

I want you so much
402 Payment Required

I want to see you
404 Not Found: Page Cannot Be Displayed

(The most likely causes are that you are not connected to the
internet or that the address you entered is incorrect)

I only want to see you
415 Unsupported Media Type

I must see you!
426 Upgrade Required

I wanna bite you
423 Locked

WTF? How I'd love to lock you up
405 Method Not Allowed

I hate you more than anything
451 Redirect

我愛你
401 Unauthorized 未經授權

愛你愛你愛你
403.11 密碼變更密碼錯誤已達三次

我愛你！！
418 I'm a teapot

O I love you
401 Unauthorized Uncommitted

Love you love you love you
403.11 You have exceeded the number of allowed attempts

I love you!!
418 I'm a teapot

繁簡轉換

繁體比簡體soft
當z在製作我們的sofa
他可以用這三個字
親愛的
繁體
一層層氣墊
包裹新刨的木料

我坐在sofa上教他
繁簡轉換的藝術
他坐在sofa上教我
我們又寫又讀
有的字容易
有的字困難
我們坐在sofa上練習
一整天不覺得疲倦

Character Conversion

Complex characters seem softer than simplified ones
when Z was making our sofa
he offered to use the former

for then the word for "beloved" has more love in it
complex characters
to cushion the newly cut wood
smooth the rough edges

I sat on the sofa teaching him
the art of character conversion
he sat on the sofa teaching me
we wrote and we read
some words were easy
others were hard
we sat on the sofa and practiced
over and over and never grew weary

冰

手伸入老虎嘴裡
探進去掏牠的心臟
我也這樣
從一本書切下
冰

好燙！

我尖起嘴
抽著蓬蓬升起來的煙

這另類療法
是住我地下室的巫婆教的
我倆長得越來越像
月經同一天開始

我沒收她租金
她教我治療
臉上兩大傷口

在靈魂被秤出淨重21g以前的古代
這兩個曾被稱作「靈魂之窗」

上個月我擦窗七次
這個月颱風季我得更加小心
「免得海水倒灌
損壞良田」

Ice

Thrusting your hand down a tiger's throat
to tear out his heart
so, too, I
cut from a book a sheet of
ice

How it burns!

I round my lips
expel a plume of smoke

an alternative therapy
the witch which lives in my basement taught me
the two of us grow more and more alike
our periods now start on the very same day

I don't take a penny for rent
she has taught me a timely cure
for curing the two gaping wounds on my face

wherein lies the soul weighing 21 grams, or so it was believed
the so-called "window to the soul"

this past month I washed them seven times
in typhoon season I must take extra care
"Lest saltwater intrusion
harm the fertile fields"

女高音獨白

劇院的門鎖死了只能從外面打開
到處是玻璃強化玻璃通過一連串撞擊測試國際認證
燈光一下亮一下暗清除記憶或至少提升它
使記憶抽象化
我女兒問我「為什麼聯合國無法修好大氣層的洞」
我說那是一首詩現在很少人讀詩別太認真
或者你必須連中樂透十次
聯合國一次也沒中
聯合國也在等
「我們有確鑿的證據表明, 平均每3000萬年, 地球物種就會
　　遭遇大規模毀滅」
　　或者最糟的時候設法使自己昏迷因為
「變慢的心跳減緩身體功能」
這叫損害控制
你得有國際觀
聽過地球村嗎
門鎖死了只能從外面打開
媽媽一直有點保留地教導你
你想到村子各處走走
首先, 你得學習不同的問候方式
碰碰臉發出波的聲音、豎起大小拇指搖一搖、右手舉高、互搓
　　鼻子
最常見的方法就是握手
伸出右手表明自己沒帶武器
上下輕晃兩三次
如果對方的袖子裡藏著東西就會掉出來
如果沒有就注視對方眼睛露出微笑
最保險的
媽媽一直有點保留地教導你
放學趕快回家
陌生人問路不要回答快點
跑到人多的地方

Soprano Solo

The theater is locked up tight and can only be opened from the
　　outside
all around crash-test-certified tempered glass
the lights go on, the lights go off, clearing memory or effecting
　　an upgrade
making memory abstract
my daughter asks how come the U.N. can't fix the hole in the
　　ozone layer?
that could be a poem I said and though not many people read
　　poetry now don't take it to heart
you'd have to win the lottery ten times over
and the U.N. hasn't won it even once
it's biding its time like the rest of us
scientists say there's irrefutable evidence of mass extinctions
　　occurring on average every 30 million years
when things get really bad we'll have to learn how to go into a
　　coma because
they say lowering your heart rate slows down your metabolism
they call this "damage control"
you have to have an international perspective
ever hear of the Global Village?
It's locked up tight and can only be opened from the outside
Momma is telling you this for your own good
you'll want to explore this village
but first you've got to learn the different ways to say hello
like shaping your mouth in an O or jiggling your thumb and
　　pinky or raising your arm
in the air or rubbing noses . . .
but the most common of all is to hold out your hand
to show you are unarmed
grasp the other person's palm and pump it up and down
to make sure they've nothing up their sleeve

到麥當勞喝飲料要嘛喝完再離開要嘛上洗手間後把剩下的
飲料倒掉以免
給人下了藥
不管是誰即使熟人媽媽好朋友隔壁叔叔員警ㄅㄟㄅㄟ阿公
哥哥爸爸都不能碰你
你的
廚房　海膽　燕子　小貓咪　你的
private parts
媽媽一直有點保留地教導你
因為聯合國也在等
在等
它一次也沒有中
不過它聰明地保留了票根
等行動, 等行動
結束後進場

then you look them in the eye and smile
just to be on the safe side
Momma is telling you this for your own good
when school gets out
don't stop to talk to strangers asking directions
but run straight to a busy street
and when you go to McDonald's and have to use the bathroom
    you want to first finish
your drink or throw it in the garbage can to make sure
no one slips you a mickey
and no matter who, not your momma's best friend, the guy next
    door or the kindly old
policeman, your grandpa, your brother, you mustn't let anyone
    touch
your
cucina your conch shell your swallow your pantry your
you-know-what
Momma is telling you this for your own good
because the U.N. is biding its time like the rest of us
waiting in the wings
it hasn't won even once
though it has wisely kept the ticket stubs
waiting in the wings for something to happen
and once it has and the dust has settled that's when they'll make
    their debut

爸爸很窮, 媽媽沒有奶

爸爸很窮, 媽媽沒有奶
「用一塊地養好多牲口」
我們低頭吃草
一點一點
拉出綠色
。
許多年以後
我們在一場電影重逢
哥演遠景的兵
弟演中景的老婦
姐姐正在倒下, 我喊
救命!因為被殺
獲得一次發言權
導演還即興演出:他解開鈕扣朝我前胸放血

一家人加起來幾近半分鐘
膠卷很貴
下了戲我們相約到公園吃便當
妹指著前方
我們跟著叫
啊台北 。。。
台北公園!
滿滿是鄉愁
即使看了那麼多電影演了那麼多還是洗不掉
這綠　這綠
我們嘴裡塞滿了草

Papa Was Poor, Mama Bone Dry

Papa was poor and Mama bone dry
a patch of dirt and all these mouths to feed . . .
we hung our heads and gnawed at the grass
what there was of it
shat green
o
A few years later
we were reunited in a film
Big Brother played a soldier, a walk-on part in a distant shot
Baby Brother an old lady at a closer remove
as Sis fell I too pretended to be hit, mewled
Help! And had our only speaking part
because I was dying
the director, in an improvisational turn, unbuttoned
my blouse and anointed me with blood
o o o
The whole scene lasted less than thirty seconds
each shot a single take
film stock being so dear
the shooting done
we flocked to the park to munch our box lunches
Sis lifted a hand toward the grassy prospect
of Taipei Park
and we all fell to thinking of home
despite all the films we've seen, the parts we've played
it won't wash out
this green, green
mouthful of grass

THE VERMONT STUDIO CENTER
TRANSLATIONS

Journey's End, Johnson, Vermont, September 2016

Oh, the bread and cheese they serve at lunch is so good. What do you call this in English?

Cheddar. You want some more?

No, but I'll have another glass of wine. What is it?

Pinot noir.

It's so much better than the one you brought the other day.

And a lot pricier.

What's a few dollars?

You're getting spoiled.

I am and I love it! Say, what took you so long? I thought you were lost or fallen in the falls.

I stopped to draw the view through the trees.

Let me see. Very nice! What else did you do on the walk up here? Oh, that's the shed we passed, across from the rotted farmhouse where we found those delicious apples. That's looking across our valley?

Yes. From the top of the hill where the road turns.

You're getting better every day, Steve, but you need to stop drawing and finish my book.

Your book? What am I, chopped liver?

Huh?

Never mind. You are going to at least put my name somewhere in the book?

Of course, I will, don't be ridiculous! But what I am saying is, when are you going to do more translations?

Who says I haven't?

You started?

I'm almost done with "Film Editing," but I have some questions.

What questions?

Like, why all the surgical metaphors?

Because editing that film was painful. Every edit was like cutting my flesh.

Isn't there a Chinese proverb about a son who fed his father his own flesh to stop him from dying?

Gegu liaoqin. That's an old saying: "Cut your thigh to cure your parent." It was the only thing the doctor said would cure his father's sickness. That his son cut off his own flesh and feed it to his father.

Ouch! Did it work?

No, he died anyway. But it's the thought that counts.

I might give a kidney to one of my parents if they were still alive, but I don't think I'd carve a chunk out of my own thigh.

That's because you're not Chinese.

But I'm surprised you find editing so excruciating. I mean, a lot of filmmakers—Eisenstein, Welles, Kubrick, the great ones—they all loved editing. It was their favorite part, the part that made filmmaking an art.

But they weren't making films about their families. I'm not just talking about the editing part. The whole process of making a film is a kind of editing. It begins before you even shoot the first shot because you're editing life. Life has a thousand angles, but you can only shoot from one angle at a time. But which one? You can't show every event, every person involved, everything they said or did. It's too much. The more you show, the more you risk boring. You can't tell the whole truth. It's impossible, so you cut this and cut that.

OK, I get that. But why did you feel you were betraying yourself? I don't understand the logic.

Because I had to move things around, twist this and bend that until all the parts fit together—they have to fit or everybody falls asleep—but then it was no longer the truth.

To tell the truth you have to lie a little.

You have to lie a lot! And that left me feeling like I betray myself.

"Betray" is a pretty strong word in English. The Chinese word is also used where we might say "forsake" or "turn your back on." How about—O, I know! "I had played false with myself."

No, that's good. I like that. Work versus play, truth versus false. That's good. Yes, do that.

Since you don't mind my changing "betray," how about letting me say "kidney" instead of "gallbladder"?

Why?

I hate "gallbladder." It's so, you know, clunky. "Kidney" chimes so much better with "cut."

But kidneys don't make bile, and I want that, uh, association. No, you can't change it. Don't change a word.

But . . .

No buts.

Slave driver!

Yes, you are my slave and I am your master, so no more talk of rewriting my work or I will cut out your tongue. So, are we done?

Yes, now that you have killed my best suggestion.

Good, so you go off and draw or whatever. I want to explore these woods. Save me some of that pinot noir. It's really quite lovely.

剪接

A

我想讓難以忍受的事情
看起來難以忍受
為了像它本來應該有的樣子
動了點小手術

又做些大的

效果好極了
大家都在哭
沒有人忍住

 B

剪完了片子
也背叛了自己

一次次遷徙
傾斜的家屋
都是在夢中
剪接完成

問題
並不是候鳥傳染給我的

C

剪著指甲和腳掌
剪著頭髮和膽囊
都不是我要剪的

Film Editing

A

Wanting that which was unbearable
to appear unbearable
just as it should be
I performed some minor surgery

some major surgery too

and made that final cut so good
everybody had to cry
not a single eye was dry

B

But in cutting down the raw footage
I played myself false

moving myself here, now there, this here, that there
until the whole teetering house of cards
that was the finished film
became something dreamt of in a delirium

a problem
I couldn't blame on some migratory bird flu

C

I didn't want to trim a single nail or lock of hair
much less cut off a heel
cut out a gallbladder

剪完哥哥剪姐姐

剪完姐姐剪妹妹
也不是我要的

所以我
我

剪爸爸

所以我
我

剪媽媽

nor was cutting brother
cutting sister
the older, the younger

so I
I

cut Papa

so I
I

cut Momma

"Everybody had to cry/ not a single eye was dry"—oh, I love that! It rhymes like my Chinese!

I stole it from Madeline, *a picture book by Ludwig Bemelmans.*

Is that OK?

You mean, can I steal a few lines? I think so. I'm sure Bemelmans won't mind, he's been dead for years. Have you read that book? It's about a little girl who lives in an old house in Paris covered with vines who has her appendix out and all the other girls become jealous.

I know that story!

You read the book?

No, I saw the movie on DVD with my students.

That's right, you teach English in an elementary school. Wasn't it terrible?

The movie? No, I loved it! And so did my students.

Any excuse not to do classwork. You know, someone translated the book into Chinese—I saw it in a bookstore in Taipei—but the Chinese didn't rhyme!

The English rhymes?

Beautifully! The entire book. That's what makes the book such a pleasure to read. They should be shot!

Who?

The Chinese translator. For not making it rhyme. So, on a brighter note—how many translations does that make? How many have I done so far?

Don't you know?

I figure you're keeping track so why should I bother? So how many translations do we have?

Nine. Maybe ten . . .

Ten! I've been translating you for years and all I've done is ten translations?

I know, you should be ashamed of yourself!

Well, think about all the poems I tried to translate!

And which you could have finished if you hadn't given up.

You think it's so easy, why don't you translate your poems into English? Give me a second.

What are you doing? Are you recording our conversations?!?

How else am I going to remember all the stuff you tell me about your poems? And all the complaints you have about my translations?

I don't complain about your work, Steve. I encourage you to improve it.

Same difference. Besides, a lot of what you say is really interesting. Like the last line in "Error 400-418," the line "418 I'm a teapot" was an April Fools' Day prank among computer programmers. A lot of that stuff is so interesting I was thinking we should include some of our conversations in the book. Or at least the juicy parts.

What juicy parts?

Like all that stuff about the guy you were necking with on the couch in "Character Conversion," when we were revising that poem the other day.

That's personal!

I don't mean the necking part. I'm talking about the cultural background, the fact that he was from mainland China, where they only know the simplified forms of the characters and can't read the traditional ones you still use in Taiwan.

No, no, no. He knows the traditional forms very well and would like to bring them back.

So, why were you teaching them to him?

Well, you know . . .

You're such a flirt! Anyway, that's not what I'm really interested in. It's the cultural stuff you said, about how one of the reasons the

Communists simplified the characters was to make it hard for new generations to read the old literature. That simplification made them, in effect, half-literate. That the reason you say the traditional characters seem "softer" is that words like "beloved" no longer have the radical for love in them, that, in a sense, they're heartless. That stuff is pure gold!

Can't you summarize this in your introduction?

I hate writing introductions! Besides, I want readers to hear your voice, to get to know you the way I've come to know you. It would be so much more interesting to read than an intro, which no one ever reads anyway . . .

I read them!

Come on, Amang. It would be so cool!

Hmm . . . I'll think about it.

Hmm . . . Well, while you're thinking, I'm recording. And while I am, I wanted to ask you what your folks did or do for a living?

They grew lemongrass to harvest citronella, an oil used in perfumes and candles and insect repellent.

Yeah, Taiwan has some pretty nasty mosquitoes—invisible, soundless, and able to fly through walls. Or at least it seemed that way when I was living in Taiwan.

Not just mosquitoes, but lice and leeches. We had a lot of them back then.

Ouch! Business must have been booming!

Not really. They had to cut their fields out of the wilderness. Lemongrass is not easy to grow, and it's backbreaking work to extract the oil, because you have to burn it and then boil it for hours and hours, strain the mixture, then boil it again. There was so much work, my parents worked in shifts. They worked like slaves. In the summers it was so hot, they would work in their underwear.

Are they still alive?

My mom is, but Papa died years ago.

What was he like?

He was very smart, cunning, tough, immoral, very ambitious for fame and fortune, but cursed by bad luck because he had—how can I say this?—there was a fatal flaw in his character.

What do you mean?

He had a very quick temper and often got into fights. One time he even killed a man and had to flee to the mountains to escape the law.

Wow! So that's why you grew up in Hualian!

Yes. But that was way back in the sixties before I was born. Hualian was a wilderness then, not like it is today, all touristy. His family had originally been quite wealthy, but his father lost everything gambling, and Papa had to drop out of school to work and make money to help the family pay expenses. I think this was one reason he got very angry. Another reason is he drank. I never saw it, but my brother said he used to beat my mom when he got drunk.

I remember there's a line in one of your poems, "Mijue shi buyao shanghai renhe yizhu zhiwu"—"The secret is not to harm any plant." Strange that he could be so nice to plants and so brutal to people . . .

Actually, Papa never said that. It was something I dreamt he said. I'm hoping that whatever heaven or hell he wound up in he's become a gentler man. I guess because he drank a lot, we never had any money. We were always very poor. We often couldn't pay the rent and had to move many times, but we were never far from the sea. Most of these places were just a few minutes from the beach.

Could you hear the sea from your house?

Of course, day and night. Especially at night.

So, you grew up with the sound of the sea in your ears.

And the sound of the mountains.

Nature was your mother tongue!

Yes! My real mother rarely ever talked to me. She rarely talked at all. If she opened her mouth, it was just to repeat something my father said, as if she had no opinion or ideas of her own. Neither of my parents was very loving. They basically ignored me. So much so that I often felt sorry for myself when I was a little girl. But looking back, I realize I wouldn't be the person I am now if I had had loving parents. Because, you know, in Taiwanese culture, most mothers become tiger moms as soon as you start school. Nag you constantly about your homework, make you cram, cram, cram. Or they stuff you with moral wisdom, all that Confucian nonsense about how girls are supposed to behave; how they should have ears but no mouths and only do what they are told to do. You have no childhood, no privacy. I escaped all that because I didn't live with my parents. Unlike my classmates, I was free to do what I liked, climb the hills, play on the beach. I read because I loved to read, not because someone told me to.

So, who did you live with? Who brought you up?

My grandmother. My father's mother. She was quite a character. She was very powerful and courageous. A she-wolf. She would do or say whatever she wanted. None of the Confucian non-sense for her. And could she swear! All my life I have never met anyone who could swear like my granny.

Swore like a sailor, did she? She ever swear at you?

Of course, all the time. But I was very wild, rarely did what I was told. She called me all kinds of things I can't repeat. I knew all the names for the hidden body parts long before my classmates did. She was my first sexual education.

That's funny. Because I never hear you use swear words.

Never! Except in a poem.

So, what saved you? What made you a poet?

What saved me? I think it was the mountains and sea. I've always felt a very close bond with Nature. That's why I like coming up here every day. I think the second thing was reading and writing. In Taiwan we don't have libraries like they do in the West and we didn't have money to buy books, but I read everything I could get my hands on. Scraps of paper someone dropped in the street. When school started I would read every one of my textbooks from cover to cover in the first week. I didn't understand most of it, of course, but I read it anyway. I would borrow my classmates' books. I read all kinds of books, from literature to science, and I loved to write about them even if I didn't understand. And I was likely to have some people give me a helping hand along the way—my grandmother, teachers, poets, friends.

Guardian angels.

Exactly.

Which poem you working on now?

"Tade shou yi jin yi song"—*"Her Fingers Kept Tensing."*

You mean, *"Wode shou yi jin yi song"*—*"My* Fingers Kept Tensing."

No, Her *Fingers.*

This time you've gone too far! You can't rewrite my poems!

I didn't rewrite anything. It says it right here: "Tade shou yi jin yi song."

You better get your eyesight checked.

Look for yourself!

她的手一緊一鬆

掌裡粉紅色軟球進行著
腹式呼吸
一邊抵抗, 一邊幫忙她
恢復
往日的「手勁」

值得慶幸:我的手勁在這一天還未
成為過去式

掌裡沒有軟東西, 沒有粉紅色
球狀的動機
我的手一緊一鬆

抵抗來自
手抱緊了自己

但不能更緊

我們叫做呼吸的那種運動
也因為不能堅持
向單一方向施力

鼻子一緊一鬆
構成了意識和感覺的
鬆緊帶
讓褲子沒有掉下去

配合著鼻子
無法醫治的癌
我的手一緊一鬆
我不明白它想幹嘛

Her Fingers Kept Tensing

as she works the pink rubber ball in her palm
laboriously breathing
resistance on the one hand helps her on the other
recover
that "grip" she had of old

a matter worth rejoicing over: my grip as yet has
no past tense

though they've nothing soft and pink and round
to motivate me
my fingers keep tensing

resistance comes from
being able to hold on tight, hold tight

but you can only hold so tight

so too this labor we call breathing
where you reach a point you can't go on
there's only one direction left you

nostrils working
composing thoughts and feelings
the elastic band
that helps you keep your pants on

the nose working in concert
with an incurable cancer

一下嘲笑?一下同情?
或只是幫忙提住褲子?

my fingers keep tensing
I haven't a clue what they are up to

Is this mockery or sympathy?
Or are they simply helping me keep my pants on?

That's *not* the title. That's line ten!

It's the first page you gave me.

No, it isn't. You must have lost a page. Let me show you. I have it on my phone. Wait, I need your hotspot.

Each day my poet takes me deeper into the forest and demands my hotspot. You should write a poem about that.

I should! Here, you see?

Shit! You're right.

Of course, I am right. I'm always right. And it's *hand* not fingers. It should be *tenses and relaxes*. I want you to be more faithful.

In Chinese you say "hand" all the time when they actually mean fingers or even arm. When you squeeze a ball it's your fingers that tense and relax. Admit it. And if you say "kept tensing," it means tense and relax. Relax is implied by the past participle.

Well, maybe so, but I want you to use both terms. Mentioning one without the other twists the meaning. I want the reader to see tension and relaxation in a dynamic balance, like breathing in and breathing out, yang and yin, death and life. Both are critical, equally dependent. You can't show favorites, Steve. And don't be so tense when we're discussing. You need to relax.

Jeesh! Are you my therapist now?

And speaking of breathing, I don't like the way you translate *fushi huxi.* Breathing laboriously means you're having trouble breathing, yes?

Well, yeah, but . . .

This is belly breathing, which is breathing deeply. We Chinese believe breathing from the lower abdomen gives you more *qi*, more cosmic essence, which gives back your energy and life force. Which is exactly what my friend needed when she got out of the hospital.

I was wondering who the "she" was. I thought it might have been your mom.

No, an old friend who got cancer. She's better now.

Look, I only said "laboriously breathing" because you describe breathing later as yundong *. . .*

And it should be in present tense here, where I describe my hand tensing, not past tense. It's more real that way, more . . . What's the phrase you taught me?

In-your-face. But how was I to know it was present tense here? Chinese doesn't have tenses and . . .

In-your-face. I want more in-your-face, if you please.

Yes, your highness. But, honestly, is there nothing you liked about this translation? You know, I spent almost two . . .

"Recovery"—*huifu.* I like that. And "rejoicing"—*qingxing.*

That's it? Two words? Two miserable words? Well, this is one miserable translator.

They're not miserable words. They're very nice words. That's why I like them. And I also like the way you translated *shou jin.* "Grip" is good. Perfect, really.

Why the quotation marks? I don't get that.

And you call yourself a translator! For emphasis! To get the reader to stop and think about "grip" metamorphically.

You mean metaphorically. Like get a grip on life or get a grip on yourself.

Yes, get a grip on yourself, Steve. But "My grip as yet has/ no past tense." That's not exactly what I wrote.

I know, but a straight translation of those lines sounds so awkward in English.

Let me be the judge for that. Come on, try me.

"My grip this day has not yet . . ." No, that's not right. "My grip this day has not yet/ Become past tense."

I like that!

No, you don't.

I do!

You only think you do. Trust me. My version has more oomph, more buck for the dollar. Think about it. Until you're dead, you live only in the present even if you're thinking about the past or future. And when you're in pain or under stress you're pretty much stuck in the present. Pain makes us present, right?

Hmm . . . Well, at least you keep "past tense." That works well in English, I think. Repeats "tense." I remember the first time I was learning English and was introduced to verb tenses. It was such a shock! Eat, ate, eaten. What horrible ideas! It was like language had been given the plague of old age, sickness, and death. It was like the fall from Eden, the fall of grace. In Chinese, every verb is immortal, eternal, for all time. Past, present, future—they mean nothing to it. Besides, why bother with tenses when you can indicate time with adverbs?

We crave clarity.

How unpoetical! Past perfect, past progressive, past perfect progressive, zero conditional, mixed conditional . . .

Do we have that tense?

Don't you know your own tenses?

I don't have to. I'm a native speaker.

Well, you would if you weren't. It was so painful to learn all those tenses and articles and prepositions, I wrote a poem, "I Am

Hurt by English *ji ruhe dui yingyu baochou.*" It's bilingual, but the English and Chinese are different. "I Am Hurt by English and How Do I Get Revenge?"

Didn't your creative writing teacher tell you to avoid the passive voice?

No, he told me to try everything. It's what poets do! We don't follow rules; we break them! And I'm going to write a poem that breaks every rule of English, every rule in book.

Every rule in English. Every rule in the book.

All these articles and prepositions! So confusing, so confining! Poetry needs room to breathe!

Lebensraum!

What?

Never mind.

Chinese is simple, so simple, it's simply poetic. When I think of all those idiotic things you have to do in English, all those unnecessary parts of speech . . .

Like what?

Articles, prepositions, verbal agreement—all those things Chinese proves you don't need to do, sometimes I, sometimes I . . .

What?

Feel sorry for you.

Can we get back to the translation?

Yes, because I really don't like the way you translate *dongji*. To me, motivation is always noun, never verb. It's a thing, it has shape, body, driving force, like a machine or a . . .

Motor. I could say motor instead of motivation. They have the same etymology.

The same what?

Origin. They have the same origin.

That's too concrete. We must have motivation.

I have lots of motivation because the sooner I finish your book, the sooner you'll stop nagging me.

I am not nagging you; I'm improving you. Look, Steve. I want our collaboration to be like a great date, not a seven-year marriage.

Ouch!

And I want you to change "I" to "fingers" to emphasize that the hands, the fingers, are doing this, not me, as if they had . . .

A mind of their own.

The tensing and relaxing was not something I willed; it happened involuntarily. Change

Yes, sir.

"Hold on tight, hold tight"—Oh, I really like the way you did that. And "labor of breathing." "Labor" is good here. Better than "work" or "exercise." Very suggestive. Every breath is new birth. I like the way you play "hand" in "resistance on the one hand helps her on the other."

Yeah, that's even better than the original, isn't it?

Careful, Steve! Don't get . . . What's the word?

Cocky.

Yes, don't get cocky. "When you reach a point you can't go on / there's only one direction left you." I like that too, but does it have the same meaning as the Chinese? I can't tell.

When you breathe in you can only inhale so far before you have to reverse direction and breathe out and so on.

Exactly.

But mine could also mean that when you can't breathe any longer they'll put you six feet under. You know, put you in the grave until you're pushing up daisies.

Good. Perfect.

I don't get the next-to-last line. Yixia chaoxiao? Yixia tongqing? *Are you saying, "Is this in mockery or sympathy?" or "Mocking one moment, sympathizing the next"?*

Both. I want you to figure out a way to say both at once.

Argh!

Come on, Steve. You can do it. I know you can.

OK, I'll sleep on it, but, you know, I got to tell you I actually like the shorter version better, the one without the opening lines. It's more of a surprise, more dramatic to start with her hand rather than yours. Do you really need all those opening lines? Why don't you let me leave them out?

Of course not. You can't change a word

How come you're free to edit my work but I can't edit yours? This is so unfair!

Life's unfair, Steve. Get used to it. So, are we done now?

No, I have some questions about the opening.

OK, but make it quick.

I'm not sure how to translate daoshang. *A literal translation, "knife wounds," makes it sound like she has been cutting . . .*

Cutting?

Cutting herself. That they were self-inflicted cuts because she was depressed or something.

No, no, no. She had surgery as part of the cancer treatment.

Ah, surgical scars!

That's too abstract, too cold, too . . .

Too surgical.

What do you mean?

No feeling. Clean. Bloodless.

Yes, I want more feeling, more blood.

I can do blood. I'll come up with something.

我的手一緊一鬆

我的手一緊一鬆
我不明白它想幹嘛

我看過回來的病患
帶著刀傷
一雙
新手
打開沒有危險標誌的家門
沉入沙發
她的手一緊一鬆

掌裡粉紅色軟球進行著
腹式呼吸
一邊抵抗, 一邊幫忙她
恢復
往日的「手勁」

值得慶幸:我的手勁在這一天還未
成為過去式

掌裡沒有軟東西, 沒有粉紅色
球狀的動機

我的手一緊一鬆

抵抗來自
手抱緊了自己

但不能更緊

我們叫做呼吸的那種運動
也因為不能堅持

My Fingers Tense and Relax, Tense and Relax

My fingers tense and relax, tense and relax
I haven't a clue what they are up to

I'd seen the invalid home
bearing the wounds where she had come under the knife
hands
she hardly knew
opening a door with no warning signs
sink into the sofa
her fingers tense and relax, tense and relax

as she works the pink rubber ball in her palm
belly breathing
resistance on the one hand helps her on the other
recover
that "grip" she had of old

a matter worth rejoicing over: my grip as yet has
no past tense

though they've nothing soft and pink and round to provide
    motivation

my fingers tense and relax, tense and relax

resistance comes from
being able to hold on tight, hold tight

but you can only hold so tight

so too this labor we call breathing
where you can't go on and reach a point

向單一方向施力

鼻子一緊一鬆
構成了意識和感覺的
鬆緊帶
讓褲子沒有掉下去

配合著鼻子
無法醫治的癌
我的手一緊一鬆
我不明白它想幹嘛

一下嘲笑?一下同情?
或只是幫忙提住褲子?

where there's only one direction left you
nostrils tense and relax, tense and relax
composing thoughts and feelings
the elastic band
that helps you keep your pants on
the nose working in concert with
incurable cancer

my fingers tense and relax, tense and relax
I haven't a clue what they are up to
cold one moment? warm the next?
or are they simply helping me keep my pants on?

• • •

Yes, this version is much better, Steve. I don't know why you
didn't make it like this at first. It would save us a lot of time.

I was hurt by your Chinese and that was my revenge.

Hmm . . .

我14你15

吃飯前牆那頭有人敲三下
什麼也沒想我朝同一面牆敲三下

是不是有人在求救？
你不去救人幹嘛敲牆回應！

我低頭扒飯
牆那頭又來三下

米飯透著收割的氣味：高音部、中音部、低音部
口水粒粒分明　。。。

你肯定赤著腳
我鞋也脫了

I Am 14, You Are 15

Through the dining room wall comes a knock knock knock
for no real reason I knock right back

might someone need help?
if you're not going to save them, why return their knock?

I hunch over my lunch
but still there comes a knock knock knock

bowl of rice bouquet of something freshly cut: head notes, heart
    notes, base notes
mouth savoring each and every grain

I bet you're barefoot
I too take off my shoe

房間的情緒

房間很煩躁
房間很憂鬱
房間有病
它飽滿的精神
反抗
空虛的肉體
房間自殺過許多次
每一次都幾乎得手
如果不是有
人
走進來
割他的血管或
吊頸子
把窗簾的尼龍繩
拉　　　　斷
其中一位醫生
從他泥水匠弟兄那兒
運來磚頭
打算把自己砌進潛意識的
酒窖
。爛電影
使房間很心煩
很氣餒
沒時間生病

The Mood of a Room

A room so annoying
a room so depressive
a room simply sick at heart
yet filled to the brim with the spirit
of resistance
to the vacuous flesh
a room which sought to end itself more than once
and would have
had not someone

stepped in
slashed his wrists
another slipped a noose around his throat
a curtain cord
so taut it   broke
as well as others, among them a physician
whose brother, a bricklayer
walled up the wine cellar
of the subconscious mind
。 A perfectly abysmal movie
that left the room distraught
so thoroughly dismayed
there wasn't time to be sick

你15我16

你說開成震動是因為手機的鈴聲很鳥
如果響起來會很囧
還沒藍芽, 傳個流行音樂也不行!

嗯, 我相信
15歲的
鳥

我也養過。現在我

左胸鈴聲比那個更鳥
帶毛帶血, 如果響起來更囧

震動也不行, 不是流出來就會掉出來

You Are 15, I Am 16

You said: I switched to vibration mode 'cause that bell-tone ring
tone's so old-hen
whenever it goes off I feel like a dodo
stupid phone doesn't even have Bluetooth so I can't share my
favorite songs!

When I was your age
I believe I had a bird
like that

I still keep close to me. But now

whenever it squawks and feathers fly
I feel even more old-hen

even in vibration mode, if not all aflutter, I'm flailing

"Old-hen" for *niu*—I like that!

That was Lisa's idea.

Good for her!

"Dodo" for jiong *was mine. I tried to keep your bird imagery, and where I couldn't I suggested it somewhere else, as in the last line.*

Good! You compensate here where you lose something there—I like that strategy.

So who is the "you"? Your daughter?

Yes, she was always nagging me to get her a new phone. Reminded me of myself when I was her age and rebellious. I've been rebellious off and on ever since, but adults aren't allowed to be rebellious, just kids. So what next?

I'm trying to translate Jianren . . .

Bitch!

I'm not sure that's how I'd translate the title, but that's not the part that has me stuck. It's the refrain, "Hao bu hao" . . .

But that's so simple, Steve—"OK?" "Alright?" "Right?"

That's what it means, but it's not how it feels or sounds.

I don't know what you mean.

Well, for one thing, it's a lovely little palindrome. You know, a phrase that you can read backwards or forwards and it sounds the same, which means the beginning of the phrase and the end rhyme with each other.

I never noticed that . . .

It's really very musical, which is why I figure you repeat it so many times and even end the poem with "hao bu hao" . . .

Yes!

I thought about it all evening. I've a whole page of different ways to say that in English. "How about it?" comes close—it even repeats the same dipthong—but it's not a palindrome. And the "it" sounds so curt and abrupt, as if the speaker were getting impatient with the reader. Anyway, I figure, if you can't translate the last line of a poem, there's no point in bothering with the rest. That's why I always start with the last line first. I'll keep working on it, but right now I'm stymied.

Perhaps we could discuss this on Thursday at the writing workshop.

Shit! I forgot about that! I better get cracking!

• • •

Wasn't that a great session!

Not bad. I liked April's suggestion to leave "Meimei" untranslated.

It sounds so much better than "Baby Sister," but do you think readers will understand what it means?

Beatrix Potter always said it's good to throw in a difficult word now and then. Challenges the mind. Besides, Americans need to start learning Chinese.

Yes! I wish we could workshop all your translations.

Don't worry. I run all my work by Lisa, and she gives great suggestions. Besides, we'll be able to workshop some more translations when Carl Phillips comes.

It's a pity we don't have workshops like that back home.

That's right, you don't have creative writing programs in Taiwan . . .

Well, actually we do have a few, but we don't have workshops like you have here. Chinese people are very thin-skinned. They don't take criticism very well. People are afraid to speak their mind because they worry they will offend.

It's true here, too. You have to be very diplomatic. Not everyone is as nice as these guys. Taylor runs a great workshop. I was in a workshop once where the guy who led it came down so hard on us that we all felt crushed, wanted to throw in the towel.

Throw in the what?

The towel. It's an expression meaning "to quit." It comes from profes-
sional boxing. If a boxer is getting really beat up his manager can stop
the fight by throwing a towel in the ring.

You're not going to throw a towel in, are you, Steve?

Don't worry, Amang. I can take a punch.

Are you sure? You did a lot of griping the other day when we were
discussing "My Fingers Tense and Relax, Tense and Relax" . . .

That's different! You hit below the belt!

Don't exaggerate.

她說

我什麼都可以給妳
妹妹
只差一小節
只差一根多出來的小指
妳在乎嗎

我會彈奏各種樂器
無論弓弦、撥弦、木管、銅管、鍵盤、打擊
相信我：我是天才！

我每天游泳4000公尺
我的月經非常漂亮
我的胸膛非常厚實
還有彈性

20年, 我喜歡妳20年
要不要考慮我的提議
要看我的裸照嗎
妳愛男人嗎
昨個晚上妳睡在男人的床上嗎
我打到妳家妳沒接電話
手機也沒開
妳整晚沒有回家
睡在哪裡

妳睡得好嗎

今早妳來過了
柔情似水

我們還做了

妹妹
妳的夜晚是我的白天

She Says

I can give you anything
Meimei
except that puny little stick
they call a prick
and is that worth making a fuss about?

I can play anything
I blow a mean trumpet and can strum with the best of them
believe me, *Meimei,* when it comes to fingering
I'm a bona fide genius

I swim four thousand meters a day
my periods are perfect
my pecs, too
and, boy, can I flex

for twenty years I've loved you, twenty years
so why not say yes
you want to see my nude photos?
Is it men you like?
Did you sleep with a man last night?
I tried calling you at home but you never answered
and your cell phone was off
you were out the whole night
where did you sleep?

Did you sleep at all?

I could have sworn I saw you just as dawn was breaking
You were tender as the morning mist
we were making love

好多的水
太平洋在我們之間湧動
好多的水

星星好多
有時我的夜晚是妳的白天
地球不轉動絕對造成災難

打開妳內心的門窗
看看你忘記的角落那口發光的箱子
我們已經浪費了20年

我不只說說而已
我已經做好長遠的計畫
幫你買機票好嗎
明年我升上教授你就過來長住
妳不想生孩子
我來生
我好想要兩個人的孩子
我來生我們兩個人的孩子
和妳一樣漂亮
和我一樣漂亮

妹妹
今天早上你來過了
雖然我根本沒有時間作春夢

嫁給我好嗎

告訴我
妳真的來過嗎

不用急著回答我
馬上告訴我

Meimei
your night is my day
all that water
the Pacific surging between us
all that water

stars galore
there are times my night is your day
if the earth stopped turning it would be disastrous

open your heart to me
unlock that chest you left gleaming in some forgotten corner
we've already wasted twenty years

this isn't just talk
I have plans for you
let me buy you a plane ticket
next year I'll make full professor and you can come to stay
if you don't want to have a child
I can have it
I want to have a child with you
I want to have a child
as pretty as you
as pretty as me

Meimei
you came this morning
though I don't have time for this

Will you marry me?

Tell me
did you really come?

don't rush to answer
just tell me right away

她說整晚找不到我我是不是和男人一起

有時我晚上和男人一起
有時和山
有時和女人
一群樹
有時有男也有女
推擠的葉
變形的石頭
有時只是走路
走了一晚
到溪裡洗頭
等陽光出來晾乾頭髮
沒和什麼一起
沒什麼特別須要交代
有時我離掉電話
關掉手機
有時我掉了出去
忘掉密碼
有時忘掉媽媽
有時我不想回家
有時我沒有帶
有時沒戴
有時跳了號
有時跳了床
有時用光了口袋
有時我懷上孩子
有時她出了櫃
有時我出了血
有時一整個晚上生, 生不出
次日清晨太陽出來
不用枝枝節節
不用砍不用鑽
就有了

She Said She Couldn't Find Me Last Night and Asked If I'd Been with a Man

Sometimes I'm with a man
sometimes I'm with a mountain
sometimes with a woman
a grove of trees
sometimes I'm with men and women
the jostle of leaves
rocks altering their shape
sometimes I walk
walk the whole night long
to wash my hair in a brook
wait for the sun to come
and dry it
I'm not actually with anything
and don't need to explain
there are times I leave the landline off the hook
turn off my cell phone
light off for parts unknown
there are times I forget all my passwords
times I forget my mom
times I don't care to go home
there are times I don't carry it
times I don't wear it
times they skip my number
times I sleep around
times I'm empty-pockets
times I'm heavy with child
now and then she'll come out of the closet
here and there I'll bleed
at times you labor the whole night through and labor in vain
to build a fire
and the very next day

火
大的
有時用來熬湯
有時熬夜
有時搗古老的草
有時春最新的藥
有時熬路
起初很淡,越來越濃
剛開始都是前腳
後來就熬出後腿
剛開始熬著黑暗
後來就煮出落葉
腐植層
有機營養
月亮
洞
鳥叫
占卜
追蹤
追蹤蹄子、獸、祖先、我
有時我晚上和白天一起
有時我旋轉
有時睡著了什麼都不能叫我起來!

without a scrap of wood
or striking a match
the morning sun will set the sky on
fire

up a savory soup
burn the midnight oil
grind up an old-fashioned potion
pound out a newfangled cure
to stew the road
till it thickens
boil up the broth of advancing feet
boil it down to the heels that follow
boil up black night

simmer the fallen leaves
loam
nutritious organic mix
moonlight
grottoes
the cries of birds
augury
tracking
hooves, beasts, paternity, me

some nights I keep day company
some days I turn

sometimes I fall into a sleep so deep that nothing can wake me

Who was she?

Just someone who had a crush on me. I wasn't interested, but she kept calling me. So I finally wrote these poems.

Love—interesting concept . . . Speaking of which, I'm thinking of doing "Kiss" next, but I have a question . . .

No, no, no! I want you to translate "Oh, If Only One Day My Memory Were Good"! I finished editing the film and I want you to translate the poem so I can have Kirsten do an English voiceover before we leave.

We have almost two weeks left. What's your hurry?

I want to finish it now so we can workshop it on Thursday.

What, you don't trust me?

I do, Steve, but as you always say, the more feedback the better.

如果有一天我的記憶力變好了

好到我不必去看你

也不想

我們可以永遠不相見
一點也不會感到遺憾

只用一天
我在倉庫裡囤積的糧食
已經足夠
對付不管多少年間
每一次突然降臨的飢荒

這些存糧不怕黑暗
不會受潮不腐爛也不發芽
（芽是有毒的）

怎麼吃都吃不完
也不膩

如果有一天我的記憶力變好了

我說過我的記性很差
到目前為止, 多少年了
我們只見過: 一次
我們只在一起: 一天
（四捨五入, 取整數計算）

那時你好像也順便提了一下
你的記性不會比我好

萬一有一天你的記憶力變好了呢

Oh, If Only One Day My Memory Were Good

So good I wouldn't have this need to see you

might not even want to

so good that if we never met again
I wouldn't have a single qualm

what I would have harvested that day
could well fill
a silo
enough to weather the longest
famine

what I would have reaped
would not fear the dark
would never decompose, grow stale, or sprout
(avoiding any chance of toxic offshoots)

would never run out
would never cloy

oh, if only one day my memory were good

I think I mentioned I've a wretched memory
in all these years
we met only once
had but one day together
(rounded off to the nearest whole number)

I vaguely recall your mentioning
your memory was worse than mine

if by chance you do remember everything one day
what then?

So, you have no qualms about my using the word "qualm" instead of "regret"?

No, I like it.

You're sure? Because once this translation goes into print, it will stay that way forever. It's not like memory. It won't decay or be rewritten in the mind.

I'm sure.

You know what Nietzsche says about memory? Or, rather, forgetfulness?

No.

That it's the key to action, a creative force. Because if you remember everything you become paralyzed by all the options there are, all the consequences. We need to forget in order to act.

That's true. If my memory were good, I probably wouldn't be a poet. Poetry is a kind of creative forgetting and rewriting.

Funny you should say that. Sometimes when I'm trying to translate a word or phrase that eludes me, I become paralyzed by the options I find in the dictionary. I know that none of them are quite right, but I can't see my way past them because there they are, staring me in the face with all the authority of the dictionary. It's when I forget the source text that a week later, a better way to render something comes to mind. Like the word "landline" in "She Said She Couldn't Find Me Last Night and Asked If I'd Been with a Man." I don't think I would have come up with that word if I hadn't forgotten the Chinese. Or "pouches" for "pockets" to get a rhyme for "couches."

I guess you could say that translation is a kind of creative rewriting, too.

The danger, though, is paraphrase. You don't want to simply ignore the text; you just want to forget it long enough to make that lateral leap.

我緊緊抱你的時候這世界好多人死

我緊緊抱你的時候這世界好多人餓死
我緊緊抱你的時候這世界好多人戰死
我緊緊抱你的時候這世界好多人發生意外, 死了
我緊緊抱你的時候這世界好多人自己幫助自己死去, 環抱自
己的手
一下子放鬆
我不抱世界這麼多沒有呼吸了的人我抱你就抱著感覺窒息
在我緊緊
也被你緊緊地抱住這時候這麼多人感覺不到
我們
瀕臨真空拔高的愛情的顫抖
潮浪
越過了石堆
那麼多現在不動聲色
被搬動的石頭
下一刻
愛
能不能
下一刻
更多不動
被搬動的石頭
沒有答案
不要
有
我知道我們能不能再互相緊緊抱著是我不知道的
或者在某個人停下來想下一個字
一顆炮彈在空中優美地畫過
一滴水飽滿地騰越
潛水艇安安靜靜
地雷乖巧
掃乾淨的地灰塵爭相落下
草籽兒精神好綠

As We Embrace Thousands Are Dying All Over
the World

As we embrace thousands are dying of starvation
as we embrace thousands are dying in wars
as we embrace thousands are dying in violent accidents
as we embrace thousands are having a hand in their deaths with
    a final hug before letting go
I can't embrace those who are no longer breathing I embrace
    you embracing me till we can barely breathe this here this
    now so many can no longer feel us
shuddering with love on the verge of being lifted into that one
    true nothingness
waves
sweeping over stony
rubble
unmoved and silent
from this moment on
will love enable
or is love unable
from this moment on
will these stones
remain so unmoved so silent?
there is no answer
I don't want an answer
but I do
I know my knowing whether we will ever be able to embrace
    like this again is a great unknown
just imagine someone pausing to consider their next word
a cannon shot tracing a graceful arc across the sky
a tiny sphere of water rising in the air
a quiescent submarine
a well-mannered land mine
the dust vying to be the first to soil a well-swept floor

你也感覺到了嗎在你緊緊抱我的時候好多人死了
你緊緊抱我的時候好多人精神錯亂走過熄滅篝火旁歪歪倒
倒營帳深深淺淺石堆
好多人流星飛過我們接著吻的窗台
你聽得到窗外的鳥
蟬
那麼多
比石器時代更久遠的石頭？

the grass seed a vigorous green
do you also feel when we're embracing that thousands are dying?
As you embrace me thousands scramble in desperation over
    dying campfires the toppled tents the mounds of stone
thousands fly like shooting stars past the window where we
    stand locked in a kiss
can you hear the birds from here
the cicadas
and all these stones
that are so much older than the Stone Age?

Are you sure you're happy with the title, Amang? "As I Hold You Tightly" is much closer to the Chinese than "As We Embrace."

No, I like the sound of it. "Embrace" is a beautiful word. It gives the feeling of *jinjin* even if it doesn't have the same meaning.

It's your call. You know, I think "War Flick" would pair nicely with this poem.

Good idea.

I started a draft last night, and I think I came up with a nice way to translate the quote. "My youth, that small bird, has flown." What is that from?

It's an old Chinese folk song called "Qingchun Wuqu."

Dance of Youth?

You've heard of it?

Nope. How's it go?

> 啊,太陽下山明朝依舊爬上來
> 花兒謝了明年還是一樣的開
> 我的青春一去無影蹤
> 我的青春小鳥一去不回來
> 我的青春小鳥一去不回來

別的那樣呦 呀
別的那樣呦
我的青春小鳥一去不回來

Ah, the sun has set, but in the morning it will rise again
The flowers have fallen, but next year they blossom as before
My youth has gone without a trace
My youth, that small bird, has flown
Never to return
My youth, that small bird, has flown
Never to return . . .

That's an awful melody, but I like that line.

I like the image—it has a Fauvist feel, a touch of the wild.
But I was actually thinking of replacing it with some lines
from an Adam Levine song called "Lost Stars," which I first
heard in a movie titled *Begin Again*.

Don't know that one either. What are the lines?

"God, tell us the reason youth is wasted on the young/ It's
hunting season and the lambs are on the run."

That's very different from the Chinese.

True, but they're both about lost youth. The Chinese is not
quite as tragic as the English, which I think is why I prefer to
quote Levine's song.

It does seem to fit better. What do you say we just quote the second line, "It's hunting season and the lambs are on the run"?

Good.

戰爭電影

電影天鵝湖都是男人
乘異色的夢從天而降
張開翅膀如飛彈炸響
忽然使追求者半裸全裸
大放光明,夢的
內褲濕透
至次日
早
。許多天鵝還賴著
青草床
床頭音響播放:「我的　青春　小鳥　　一去
不　　　回　　頭……」
這天鵝之歌,再也
不能給麗達,他們的麗達
用鵝毛筆寫信了

有一些淚溢出床單
手帕從湖裡舉起
有一些還是眼睛
還沒有
扣下扳機。有一些
在電影裡看
電影
還在想怎麼去愛
什麼姿勢如何
不要太笨拙第一次
有一些沒有殺人
有一些還是處男

天鵝之歌放送完就是字幕
就是一些字一些淡淡的水紋

War Flick

This version of *Swan Lake* has an all-male cast
a dream suffused with a pornographic glow
falling from heaven
the explosive blast of great wings beating
half stripping the suitors of their clothing
in a burst of light, a dream
down to its drawers, wet
in the darkness before
the dawn
a ballet of swans lingering
in the rushes
the bedside stereo blaring, "*It's hunting season and*

the lambs are on the run . . ."
this swan song for Leda
their Leda, will never
be written with a goose quill pen

tears spill from the bedsheets
handkerchiefs rise from the lake
some are still eyes
yet to
pull the trigger. Some
watching a flick
within a flick
are still wondering how to love
pondering the best position
to rise to that first occasion
some have never killed
some are still virgins

after the swan song the closing credits
a smattering of lines, a few faint ripples

雪

雪下了很久

雪不想見到
有些屍體

有些謀殺
雪決定遮蔽

雪藉有些腳呼吸
藉有些腳喊叫

雪買進一些腳
賣出一些

雖然很小而且沒有很多
從這筆交易雪賺到有些眼睛

雪從眼睛看出去
那麼多大東西

更多更大的東西
雪還沒有蓋住

雪越下越久
把自己暴露
在越來越危險的地方

Snow

Snow has been falling for a long time

there are dead
snow does not care to see

there are willful murders
snow resolves to hide from view

there are feet snow can breathe through
it can cry out through

feet the snow buys into
feet the snow sells off

though the sums are small, the trade infrequent
snow profits in the currency of eyes

eyes the snow can see through

things looming

dwarfed by still more massive things
snow has yet to cover

snow—the more it falls the more it feels like it will fall forever

exposing itself
in ever more perilous places

Very clean, Steve.

Like the snow.

今天的雨

今天的雨
不是被想要的雨
她下著媽媽的舌頭
赤裸裸
沒有加密
從我們看膩了的雲

今天的雨
她沒有說好聽的新鮮的
讓我們一聽就熱機了的
像Siri會講的那種話

今天的雨
她下著媽媽的舌頭
重重的, 腫腫的

她問我
一個蠢問題:

你要選
可以吃的蘋果還是
不可以吃的蘋果?

The Rain Today

The rain today is not the rain one longs for
She showers us with mother tongues
Raw
Unencrypted
From clouds we've long grown weary of

The rain today
Does not regale us with sexy new phrases
That fire up our engines
The way Siri does when she does what she does

The rain today
Showers us with mother tongues
Heavy, inflated, inflamed

She asks me
A silly question

Do you prefer
An apple you can eat
Or an apple you can't

是的, 愛人, 我一直形而下

不要問我哪個會先掉
不要問我地心引力更愛誰
有雲就會下雨嗎

今晚你用眼睛看見了。最好。你和我可以永遠不必開始
用口
瀟灑這波那波試圖脫離地心引力的口水
今晚我用力丟我
是肉先落地
是肉

Yes, Lover, I'm Always This Physical

Don't bother asking who will be the first to fall
or which of us gravity loves most
when clouds rear, is it a given rain is near?

This evening you saw it with your very own eyes. Which is best.
    You and I need never

wax
salivic in a bid to keep gravity at bay
this evening I flung myself away
the flesh was first to fall
flesh

Kiss

在我和這匙蜜
之間
沒有蜜蜂細得足以穿越

即使蜜蜂的夢也不行
即使一隻正在作夢的蜜蜂
牠吹玻璃一樣吹長嘴裡的彈簧吹著每朵花開, 吹, 吹
吹出了整座花園

如果這時有人伸手關掉世界
唯一的嗡嗡聲
發自我和honey . . .

Qinwen

Between me and this spoonful
of honey

there is no honeybee small enough to pass
or even the dream of a honeybee
or a honeybee dreaming
of unfurling its tongue like a glassblower trumpeting flower after
     flower
a garden in bloom

if someone were to turn off the world
the only sound you'd hear would be
the humming
coming from me and my honey spoon

You changed the title?

Yes. I thought if you can use the English word for "kiss," I can use the Chinese.

Hmm . . .

植物學

二月
河床擴張；卷鬚蔓延
水開了
花
我們對植物的研究進入
田野的實地調查
「水花淤積的地方就是河床」
伸出綠手指，你朝河床邊畫
邊寫：
圓構成水
三角構成花
圓和三角互相滲透、組織、
淤積

二月，我們到沖積的田野採集

Botany

February
expanse of riverbed, river bottom; tendrils spread
water comes to a boil
blooms
and so we begin our botanical inquiry, enter into the spirit of it
survey the lay of the land
"The place where it blooms, where it silts up is the riverbed"
extending your hand, your green thumb, you face the bed and
    paint a picture
as you write:
circles make water
a triangle a flower
their mutual penetration brings a new order to things
rich deposits

February, we sample the alluvial fields

I really like the way you translated that, Steve. "Water comes to a boil/ Blooms"—very beautiful.

Did you know that "a boil" is the word we use to describe water where it wells up over a fresh water spring?

No, I didn't. What a coincidence!

There's a big one at the Ichetucknee Headsprings, in Fort White, where I swim every evening.

You'll have to take me there when we go to Florida next week.

So, is this poem about what I think it's about?

Yes!

Why do you always hide your story under another story? Why don't you say it straight for once?

What's the fun in that?

Hmm . . . So, your boyfriend is a botanist? I thought he was a climber.

That's none of your business.

Everything is my business. I'm your translator.

Not for long if you keep asking me personal questions.

What if you win the Nobel Prize one day? All the reporters are going to come flocking to my door and the first thing they're gonna ask is who you're sleeping with. What am I gonna tell them?

You can tell them I was raised by wolves and never sleep.

Do they have wolves in Taiwan?

No. But that's why we're so dangerous. Because people don't think we exist until we have them by the throat.

You should write a poem about being raised by wolves. You're so feral. How can you walk around barefoot on all those rocks without screaming?

Practice.

THE COVE PARK / MELROSE TRANSLATIONS

*Cove Park, Scotland / Melrose, Florida, May 2018,
via Line Messenger*

Hello, Amang? So nice to hear from you!

Is this a good time to call?

Yes, but what are you doing up at 3:00 a.m.?

It's not 3:00 a.m. It's 8:00 p.m. I'm in Scotland.

You got the residency!

Yes, I arrived a couple days ago. It was very warm the first day, but it has been cold and rainy ever since. You don't mind if I eat while I'm talking to you?

No, not all.

I missed happy hour, but they saved me a half bottle of wine.

I'm so glad you called, Amang. I've been feeling very guilty about not finishing your book.

Our book!

Yes, of course. So many things came up, and the more I put it off, the harder it was to pick up again.

I'm here for four weeks and have plenty of time. Maybe we can finish it now. I think we only need five or six more poems.

Did you write a title poem?

No. I keep thinking about it, but nothing yet.

I hear they have wolves in Scotland. Maybe that will inspire you. In the meantime, I'll look through As We Embrace *and find something short to start with.*

Great! I'll call you at the same time tomorrow. The only place their signal is strong is in the common room, so we'll only be able to talk at certain times.

. . .

Hey, Amang!

I'm having a glass of wine. It's my third glass today.

You're becoming a lush!

It's still raining and I'm so cold. I should have bought some Scotch at the airport. There aren't any stores for miles! Did you finish a translation?

I did! I texted it to you a few hours ago.

Great! Let me read it.

這是我留在相片外的原因嗎

我對到他的眼睛的時候
他正在一張相片裡頭
那不是他最遠的旅行
也不是我的
但有種震動
讓我寫下
"像切入乳酪蛋糕
碰到了餅乾底"

Is This Why I Stayed outside the Frame?

When our eyes met
He had just stepped into the picture
It was not the farthest he had come
Nor the farthest I had gone
But something moved me
To write these lines:
"Like cutting cheesecake
And arriving at the crust"

Not bad!

Just "not bad"? Not "good"?

It's very not bad.

Hmm . . . Why the cheesecake imagery?

Because I love cheesecake. I love the contrast between the soft cheese and the hard crust. They're both so delicious, but you wouldn't like the one without the other because the cheese would be too sweet by itself. You would get sick of it if it weren't for the crust, which would just be a biscuit except for the cheese. It's a perfect pairing.

A marriage made in heaven, like peanut butter and jelly or poetry and translation.

You're a marriage broker, Steve!

Yeah, yeah, yeah . . . The reason I'm asking is that I wanted to know if you knew that "cheesecake" is an old slang term in English for describing scantily clad young ladies in sexy poses. The kind of thing adolescent boys pin behind their bedroom doors so their moms won't see them.

Is that what you had on your door when you were growing up?

I had a portrait of the Virgin Mary, by Leonardo!

Liar!

Yeah, yeah, yeah, can we stay focused for once?

Alright.

I thought maybe he was someone you met online. That you sent him a sexy photo and he responded by sending you one in return.

Of course not! I don't think you understand this poem at all!

Frankly, I don't. That's why I'm asking questions. So, who was this guy and why do you have his photo?

It doesn't matter! I never met him! I only saw him in a photo and fell in love at first sight.

Did you try to contact him?

No, it would be pointless. He lives much too far away.

How far?

Look, Steve, it was an old photo from a hundred years ago from the other side of the world. He's been dead for years. He probably died before I was born. But he was alive in that photo, in those eyes. His soul was in that photo.

You know what Leonardo said. The eyes are the windows of the soul.

It's true, but I've got to go pick up a delivery. It's the only way you can get anything here.

. . .

Did you start a new translation?

No, I was too busy revising "Is This Why I Stayed outside the Frame?"

What's wrong with it?

Well, after you said you didn't like it . . .

I never said I didn't like it!

. . . to amp up the musicality. Get more rhyming and chiming going on, like the original.

What did you change?

Well, I moved the phrase "he had just" up to the end of the first line, to form an end rhyme with the last line. Is that OK with you?

Sure, why not?

I also changed "It was not the farthest" to "This wasn't the farthest" and added the word "nonetheless" to increase the alliteration there. Finally, I replaced "write" with "compose" to create a kind of cascading word chain to give the last line more closure: come, compose, cutting, coming, crust.

Read it aloud!

> Is This Why I Stayed outside the Frame?
>
> When our eyes met he had just
> Stepped into the picture

This wasn't the farthest he had come
Nor the farthest I had gone
But something moved me nonetheless
To compose these lines:
"Like cutting cheesecake
And arriving at the crust"

Much better!

· · ·

Amang, it's almost 7:30! Where were you? I waited for hours.

Sorry, but I had an adventure! That's why I'm late. It finally
stopped raining so I took a walk down by the loch. I was taking
some video footage when suddenly a police car drove up and
two policemen came out and told me to stop shooting. They
asked me who I was and demanded to see my passport. Then
they took my video camera and deleted one of the videos!

Why?

Because there is a submarine base here, and nuclear silos! I had
no idea! It looks like nobody lives here but a few farmers, but it's
really a giant military base! You think you are alone, but some-
one is watching everything you do!

*They probably thought you were a spy from mainland China pretend-
ing to be a poet. Did they ask you to recite a poem to prove you were a
poet?*

No, I don't think they have interest in poetry. Did you make any progress on a translation?

I spent the whole morning on "I Just Can't Get My Head around Those Women Who Leap from Buildings," but I finally gave up. Too many lines I can't make work in English.

What a pity!

Don't worry, I'll keep at it. I'll call you if I have something to show you.

• • •

Amang, good news! I figured out a way to translate "hao bu hao" . . .

Great!

"What do you say."

About what?

About using "what do you say" for "hao bu hao" in "Jianren"!

Oh, I see! You're working on that again. Good! So, what's your solution?

"What do you say."

I like that!

I thought you would. It's not a palindrome, but it fits in like a key syntactically, with better closure.

What do you mean?

Unlike the other options, "what do you say" is not just asking for the listener's approval; it's inviting him or her to say something in return. This is an ending that invites a new beginning.

Oh, I like that! How much do you have left to translate?

I'm pretty much finished except for the title and a few lines.

What's wrong with "Bitch"?

Well, for one thing, it's very demeaning.

So is "*jianren*."

But "bitch" implies a spiteful woman who loves to complain or a female dog. "Jianren" doesn't have any of those connotations, and is gender-neutral to boot. If I used it, readers might think you or I thought women were trash. Hey, that might work!

What might work?

Trash! The adverbial form has sexual implications, as in, "Let's get trashy." Which is exactly what you say in the poem—"yiqi dang jianren!"

I like that! Send me the translation when you're done. I've got to go. We're having a barbecue.

So, how was the barbecue?

Delicious! But I drank too much. I took a long walk this morning to clear my head.

Did you have any adventures?

Yes, I got lost! You know, I don't have signal here, so I can't use my GPS. I had no idea where I was or which direction to go and it was terribly cold and foggy. But then this very nice man who used to work at the submarine base stopped and asked me if I needed help. When I told him I was staying at Cove Park and very lost, he bought me a hot lunch and drove me back to the residency. Did you finish translating "*Jianren*"?

The words aren't coming. Maybe I should work on something else for a while, clear my mind. Hey, but don't you have a poem about your GPS in "As We Embrace"?

Yes!

Send it to me and I'll see if I can translate it.

How come you're calling so late? Did you get lost again?

Not exactly, but I did have an adventure. I was trying to find a way down to the sea. I wandered around for an hour, and then this nice young guy walking his dog took me down to the beach. He works at the submarine base, too. His dog was very cute. It tried to eat the seaweed. The beach is covered with it. The water is very cold, but I took my shoes off and waded in it. I saw lots of seabirds.

See any wolves?

No!

Write that poem!

Translate "GPS"!

GPS

沒有方向感
又不信任GPS......我
亂糟糟的活

......經常錯過垃圾車

狂喜時我不在乎。因為我能

雕塑垃圾
和我之間的引力

函數。曲線。
愛情。性。

絕望時我綁住自己雙手雙腳
豎起兩顆眼睛
躺倒在白色軌道
等火車

引進海水。呼嘯

切斷垃圾和我之間
無上甚深
波羅蜜多

他們會打開我的包包。衣櫃。冰箱。銀行户頭。電腦檔案。隨身
碟。我的同事。我的朋友。家人。愛人。詩。噴泉。

檢查冰庫裡我封存的
垃圾。零下十七度
還活?還等比級數地進行無性繁殖

GPS

I've no sense of direction
    and do not trust my GPS . . . my
    life is a perfect mess

. . . I often miss the garbage truck

when I'm on Cloud Nine
I couldn't care less. For I can

sculpt the attraction
between garbage and me

The function. The curve

The love. The sex.

When I'm in the dumps I bind my hands and feet

prick up my eyes
lay me down on a white train track
and wait for a night-bound express

to return me to the sea. The whistle
to cleave the garbage and me

infinite profundity

Paramita

They will go through my bags. Wardrobe. Refrigerator. Banking
    accounts. Computer files. Flash drives. Colleagues. Friends.
    Family. Lovers. Poetry. Springs and fountains.

找我的GPS。GPS

報告長官。到處翻過了
沒有

我繼續等火車, 微笑了一下

Examine the garbage I've sealed
in the freezer. Can garbage go on living at 17 degrees below 0
Celsius? It can and it awaits exponential growth through asexual
    reproduction

they look for my GPS. GPS

report to their superiors. Though they've rifled through every-
    thing
they haven't found a trace

meanwhile, I wait for that train with a smile on my face

Wow, that was fast!

It practically translated itself. I ran it through Google Translate and then simply tweaked it. It only took a couple hours. Google is going to put me out of a job soon.

Well, you better hurry then and finish our book!

Yeah, yeah. I'm working on it. I hope you don't mind my adding the phrase "night-bound" to train in "GPS."

Why did you do that?

Because no one is going to know that white is the color of death unless they're Chinese. Night at least suggests death in English and rhymes with white, to make up for some of the rhymes I've lost.

Hmm . . . Let me think about it.

That's my line! You steal all my best lines.

That's what poets do, Steve.

I have a question: why all the periods in that long list of appliances and garbage and stuff?

To slow the reader down, to isolate the words. Each one of these things has its cache of secrets, a source of mystery that deserves individual attention. I thought you were a poetry teacher!

I'll pretend you didn't say that. Why the reference to minus 17 degrees Celsius?

Because that's the coldest you can make a freezer go.

Really? I didn't know that.

You should read more science, Steve.

I'm too busy cleaning up your garbage. Speaking of which, you sure write a lot of poems about garbage.

It's everywhere! You can't get away from it! Finish "Trash"!

賤人

我很濕了。一想到時間是人第一妄念，計時器
乃威力
最強鴉片。路邊
撿起半個信仰都能擰出水。它破得很好看
發酵得甚莊嚴。我更濕了

你和我一起
好不好

我們一起
當賤人
好不好

如果你問，永遠是什麼。我搗
我的火
小。只問你：

一個半永遠

加
一個半永遠

好不好

Trash

I get so wet. Whenever I recall that Time was mankind's first
    wild fancy, that every timepiece
is power
the strongest opium there is. But juice can be squeezed
out of every half-baked conviction gleaned along the way.
    They're so beautifully broken
and the longer they ferment the graver they get. Which makes
    me wetter yet.

What do you say
to our getting together

what do you say
to our getting trashy together

but if you mention forever, I would
dampen
my fire. And would ask you in return:

What do you say

to our adding
forever and a half

to
forever and a half

What do you say

I like it!

I'm glad you do, but I gotta tell you, I'm still a little confused.

About what?

Time, the great leveler, about why you find it so sexy.

Because it's mysterious. Mysterious things are always sexy because you don't know what they are or what they're capable of. Like a good-looking guy you meet in a bar. Or like all those fragments of Greek and Roman statues you find in museums. You can't quite believe in them, but you can't help admiring them because they're so beautiful and ancient. At the same time, I hate Time. I hate all these big abstractions. Like social harmony, family, marriage. Most of these ideas are only made by men to enslave women anyway. And men themselves too! Like the idea that you can only love one person and have to love them forever. Forever is bullshit! There is only the present!

Come out of your shell, Amang . . .

I'm not joking. Ideas like this make me wish I lived in prehistoric times. Before they invented Time. The problem is, if you only live in the present, you're little more than an animal.

Aren't you contradicting yourself?

Of course I contradict myself, Steve. I'm a poet!

You sound like Walt Whitman.

I doubt I sound like anyone else.

But what you say is a contradiction. You know that, right?

I don't know anything of the sort.

Look, first you say that Time is sexy and exciting, that it turns you on, but now you're telling me that you hate this idea, that's it's basically a form of power designed to enslave . . .

That is not a contradiction, Steve. That is how power works. It's because these bullshit ideas are so sexy that we allow ourselves to be enslaved. And that's why, in the poem, I invite other women—men, too—to get trashy, to do all the things that embarrass people in power. To ignore all the rules about how we should act. It's the one form of resistance they really don't know how to deal with, to laugh in their face.

Steve, I only have a week left. It would be really nice if you could do a few more translations for the book.

I was thinking of translating "Pixelization," but I don't understand the first line. Why "36 restrictions"? Is that just a synonym for many or are you referring to something specific?

In Chinese we have the phrase *shibajin*—the 18 restriction, "Content Forbidden for People Under 18."

Like our NC-17 film rating, "No One 17 and Under Admitted."

Exactly. I just doubled the number to show my frustration at all the restrictions there are now forbidding this and forbidding that. And to show my anger at all the vicious, small-minded people that are manipulating us behind the scenes, trying to cover everything up, the black hand you never realized was there until you see the blood on the wall.

OK, so I'll say "NC-36" for the first line and "No One 18 and Under Admitted" and so on.

Can't you say "R-18" for line two and "R-Above-18" for line three?

R-18 is a British thing. Most readers here won't know what it means. We could say "NC-17" and "NC-Above-17," but then I'd have to change "NC-36" to "NC-34."

I would prefer you use 18, because I don't just mean films. I mean all those things we aren't allowed to do until we turn 18—drink, smoke, rent a hotel room . . .

Have sex . . .

I thought 16 was the legal age for consensual sex?

Not in Florida. They're very conservative here. But I have a couple other questions. Do you mind if I add a phrase or two after Mazu to explain who she is? No one here is going to know unless they're Chinese.

Can't you use a footnote?

I hate footnotes. They're like a road sign saying, "Proceed with caution, this translation is defective!" It will also allow me to add a rhyme or two to help compensate for some of the musicality I've lost in adjacent lines.

I see.

The other liberty I'd like to take is to translate your double entendre "bai bai" as "in a white rush"—this will suggest the literal meaning of the phrase—and add "to no end" to the next line to convey the primary meaning. The first is from Yeats's "Leda and the Swan."

Yes, of course! I love that poem! I think that works well.

馬賽克

36禁:

18歲以下不准
18歲以上
不准

這最嚴厲的臉

直逼耶穌
媽祖

那隻手離開了

牆上
它打死的蚊子的血

從前不覺得這面牆這麼白。從前的時光
白白
浪費掉了

不過一開始
我只是要說小時候我們也玩過
跳格子遊戲
從這格到那格, 很容易
到達天空

Pixelization

NC-36:

No One 18 and Under Admitted
No One 18 and Over
Admitted

the strictest face of all

coming up fast on Jesus no less
and Mazu, Princess of Heaven, Goddess of the Sea

where that hand left

the wall
there lay the blood of a mosquito it had killed

on a wall I never noticed could be so white. Time passes
in a white rush
squandered to no end

though as soon as it began
I only meant to say when I was young I liked to play
hopscotch
hopping from this square to that it was easy as pie
to reach the sky

I wasn't sure if you wanted me to translate "tiankong" as "heaven" or "sky" . . .

No, "sky" is good.

Did you know that in Norway hopscotch is called paradise?

No, I didn't.

My mother told me that.

What a coincidence! So, what are you going to work on now?

I don't know. Send me some poems you wanna include and I'll take a crack at 'em.

. . .

Did you like anything I sent you?

I love "Eating Fish"!

I thought you were a vegetarian!

Hahaha . . . No, I really like that poem and want to translate it, but I have some questions.

What don't you understand?

It's not that I don't understand the poem. I'm just curious about the background. Like, who is Ah Mi?

Ah Mi is a poet friend of mine who posted a poem about her mom online. It was a very short poem that said, more or less, that after her mom was cremated they kept half the ashes for the family shrine and threw the other half into the sea, where they will no doubt be eaten by fishes we may one day eat. Which inspired me to write this poem saying how much I love eating fish, but that I can't eat fish now without thinking of all the mothers I'm eating, that we'll all wind up eating each other eventually.

Ah, the Polonius Syndrome!

The what?

In Hamlet. *You've read that play, right? It's basically what Hamlet says when the king asks him where Polonius is: "A man may fish with the worm that hath eat of a king, and eat of fish that hath fed of that worm."*

I remember the worm, but I forgot about the fish.

I was kinda hopin' that Ah Mi was a double entendre, that you were also saying, "Oh my!" or "Oh me!"

Not exactly, but close. "Ah" is what we Taiwanese say when we don't understand something. But it's also something we add to someone's name when we feel close.

But I didn't think spreading the ashes of the deceased was a Taiwanese thing.

It's not really. But it's becoming more and more popular among young people because burial plots are becoming so expensive.

You think we should mention that the Pacific Ocean, where Ah Mi spread her mother's ashes, is not very peaceful, and that the word for a morgue or mortuary is the "Pacific Room"?

I think we just did!

吃魚

早餐我吃魚
午餐我吃魚
晚餐我吃魚
我幾乎天天吃魚
不吃魚會癢
阿鏡說, 我吃了阿米的媽媽～
阿米媽媽的骨灰撒入太平洋幾年了
這幾年我吃了不知有多少
太平洋的魚
都好吃
魚鱗有閃光
魚死的時候閃光不見了, 化入肉裡頭
我就愛吃那閃光
阿米吃魚時想起媽媽
自從讀了阿米的詩, 我吃魚也想著媽媽
想著兩個媽媽
有時更多。。。
阿米的媽媽
究竟我的齒舌有沒有觸及她的靈魂?
還有那些比靈魂鹹的
還有, 不伊樣的閃光
還想著
我的媽
媽躺在醫院裡
再過幾年我可能也會吃著掉進太平洋的媽～
阿米也會吃
我的媽
阿鏡阿廖阿鈍阿發阿喊阿崔
還有不那麼阿
但也愛吃魚的
都在吃著
嗯嗯。很有滋味

Eating Fish

I eat fish for breakfast
I eat fish for lunch
I eat fish for dinner
I eat fish most every day
for when I don't I soon begin to itch
Ah Jing said I ate Ah Mi's mom.
been years since they threw her ashes into the Pacific
just think of all the fish I have eaten from that sea
every one delicious
fish scales scintillate
but when a fish dies that flash disappears, becomes flesh
a flash I love to eat
whenever Ah Mi eats fish she thinks of her mom
even wrote a poem on the subject which makes me think of
    mine
I think of both our moms
and sometimes other moms as well
Ah Mi's mom
has her soul been on my tongue?
and what of those saltier than souls
those flashes with a delicate distinction
yet still my thoughts return to
Mom
lying in that hospital ward
in a year or two I may well be eating her
and Ah Mi will be too
and Ah Jing and Ah Liao and Ah Tun and Ah Fa and Ah Han and
    Ah Cui
and all the others who are not so Ah
but love to eat fish
we'll all be eating fish one day
"Mmm," we'll say. "So savory"

Mmm. . . I like the play on "flash" and "flesh"—very clever!

Yes, I'm rather proud of that. Do you realize we have a theme going here?

What theme?

Garbage. Or rather, recycling. You read a poem and write a poem that recycles the topic, and I recycle your poem into an English translation. We're all recycled garbage.

No, Steve, we're trash, and we're sexy!

So, are we finally done now? I think we have thirty poems.

Twenty-nine. I want you to translate "Jiu Mama."

Not another poem about your mom!

What's wrong with my mom?

How do I know? I never even met her. But all these poems about family. It's so Chinese! I thought you were raised by wolves . . .

Come on, Steve. You'll like this poem. It's full of wordplay and music. Like a nursery rhyme.

Well, I'll look at it, but no promises.

Well, what do you think? Can you translate it?

I don't know, Amang. You've got so many friggin' rhymes. It's like a playground song.

I thought it was easy to rhyme in English.

Are you kidding? It's not like Chinese, where every word ends with a vowel or nasal sound. It's hard not to rhyme in Chinese, whereas in English, a lot of words have only a handful of rhymes. And what am I going to do with the repetition of the onomatopoeic "gulu gulu"?

Don't you have words like that in English?

Of course we do— "glug-glug." It's perfect for describing your sister drowning in the brook, but airplanes don't make that sound, at least not in English. They go "vroom!" or "zoom!" or "swish!" "Swish" might work for all three places . . .

That doesn't sound anything like "*gulu gulu.*" Isn't there something else you could say and still use "glug-glug"?

Gurgle? Grumble? Rumble? Hey, that might work!

Rumble?

For the plane . . .

It's a *model* plane, Steve. Not a bomber. And I don't want the brook to grumble. It's a happy sound. What do brooks say in English when they're happy?

They babble or murmur. Hey, there might be something there . . .
Murmur? Mumble? Rumble? You already nixed that . . . Burble?
Bubble? Blabber? Blubber? That might work for your sister drowning. To
blubber means to cry aloud, like a child, to boil and seethe. But none of
those sound anything like a model airplane.

I really like "glug-glug." Can't you think of something?

I'll work on it.

It seems like you have a lot more sound-words in English than
we do in Chinese. Do you think that is because English is
spelled more phonetically?

Maybe. But I think it has more to do with cultural differences. Wit and
wordplay are a lot more common in English-speaking cultures than in
Taiwan or China.

Really? Are you sure?

Do Chinese parents talk baby talk with their newborn infants or read
picture books to their kids or encourage them to read comic books?

I did! With my daughter . . .

Yeah, but you're an exception. You're a poet. Did your parents? Does the
average Chinese parent?

No, not at all.

Do they encourage kids to tell jokes or recite nonsense rhymes at the dinner table?

Of course not—that would be disrespectful.

Wit and language play are like a language. You don't become really fluent in it unless you start at an early age and do a lot of it. Chinese kids spend their childhood doing homework. I spent mine reading comics and goofing off all day so I could become your translator.

• • •

I was thinking about what you said yesterday, Steve, about Chinese not having a lot of sound-words. Actually, we do have them. You can see it in the classical poetry. The classical dictionaries are full of them. It's just that we don't use them anymore.

Too much Confucianism. Chinese needs more nonsense.

We do! Did you come up with anything that rhymes?

I did, but I'm not sure you're going to like it. I'm not sure I like it either, but it's the only thing I can think of: "chug-chug" for the plane and" zug-zug" for the brook.

What's "zug-zug"? I never heard of that.

A zug is a person who mumbles unintelligibly. It's not a verb, so we'd be doing something new. But, hey, that's what poets do—they make shit up, just like you said . . .

Hmm . . .

Otherwise, I think we're going to have to use different words, and lose the rhyme.

Maybe you should ask Lisa and see what she thinks.

Hmm . . . By the way, how come you have a period at the end of the line that says, "I only remember"?

What line?

Line fifteen: "wo zhi shi jide."

To emphasize and because Chinese period looks like a knot that we use to remember things in ancient times.

I'll try to remember that.

Then you should tie a knot!

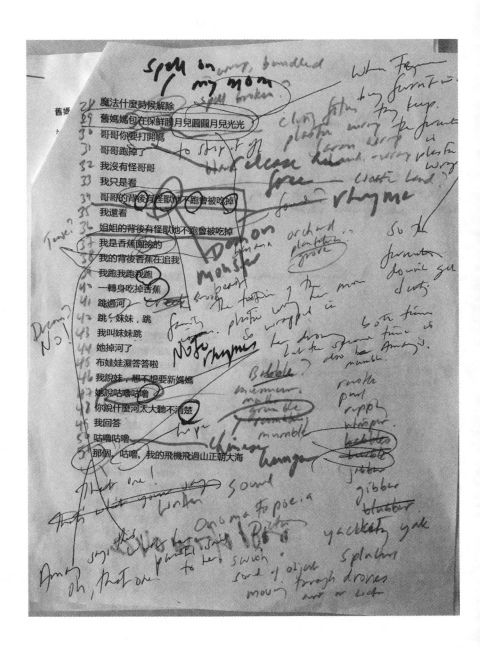

舊媽
十

28 魔法什麼時候解除
29 舊媽媽包在保鮮膜月兒圓圓月兒光光
30 哥哥你要打開嗎
31 哥哥跑掉了
32 我沒有怪哥哥
33 我只是看
34 哥哥的背後有怪獸他不跑會被吃掉
35 我還看
36 姐姐的背後有怪獸她不跑會被吃掉
37 我是香蕉園險的
38 我的背後香蕉在追我
39 我跑我跑我跑
40 一轉身吃掉香蕉
41 跳過河
42 跳，妹妹，跳
43 我叫妹妹跳
44 她掉河了
45 布娃娃濕答答啦
46 我說妹，想不想要新媽媽
47 她說咕嚕咕嚕
48 你說什麼河太大聽不清楚
49 我回答
50 咕嚕咕嚕
51 那個，咕嚕。我的飛機飛過山正朝大海

Lisa doesn't like "zug-zug." Says we should just transcribe the Chinese since it's a virtual anagram of "glug-glug"—you know, the same sounds and letters only scrambled.

I like that idea! Do it!

Thy will be done. She also said "chug-chug" sounds too much like a choo-choo train or a tugboat, and I think so too. She suggests we use "vroom!" instead, but I prefer "putt-putt." Sounds small but brave.

I like it! That's me!

舊媽媽

妹妹成天吵著要布娃娃
半個月後阿嬤縫給她
我想要電動飛機
幾年後叔叔從台北買給我
我還想要一個
新媽媽
想了幾十年不敢告訴人
為什麼不敢告訴
因為舊媽媽其實很新
幾十年都沒有用過
阿嬤縫的布娃娃還可以
軟軟的可以抱
就是不會眨巴眼睛
我的飛機飛過兩次
哥哥拆解了裝不回去
我沒有怨恨哥哥
我只是記得。
我還記得幾十年我想要
一個新媽媽
會眨眼睛可以抱
用手去指月亮會被割耳朵
小時候大人都這麼說
第一次我左耳被割第二次右耳
第三次魔法失靈
我用手指著舊媽媽
一次兩次三次
四次五次七次
魔法什麼時候解除
舊媽媽包在保鮮膜月兒圓圓月兒光光
哥哥你要打開嗎
哥哥跑掉了
我沒有怪哥哥

Old Mother

When Meimei clamored for a doll
Granny made her one in no time at all
I wanted a model aeroplane that could fly
two years went by before Uncle went to Taipei to buy me one
I also wanted a brand
new mother
wanted one for years and years but never told anyone
didn't dare tell a soul
because the old one was almost like new
hadn't been touched for years
the doll Granny stitched is still
soft and cuddly
though it still can't blink
my aeroplane flew only twice
Big Brother took it apart but couldn't put it together again
I didn't hate him
but I remember even now。
And I remember how for years and years I wanted
a new mother
one who blinked and would hold me in her arms
don't point at the moon or she'll chop off your ear
the grownups would all say
the first time I pointed she clipped my left ear, the second time
    the right
but the third time the charm didn't work
I pointed a finger right at my mom
once twice thrice
four times five times six times seven
wondering what would lift the spell
that kept her wrapped in plastic cold and shiny as the moon
I asked my brother to take it apart
but he only took to his heels

我只是看
哥哥的背後有怪獸他不跑會被吃掉
我還看
姐姐的背後有怪獸她不跑會被吃掉
我是香蕉園撿的
我的背後香蕉在追我
我跑我跑我跑
一轉身吃掉香蕉
跳過河
跳, 妹妹, 跳
我叫妹妹跳
她掉河了
布娃娃濕答答啦
我說妹, 想不想要新媽媽
她說咕嚕咕嚕
你說什麼河太大聽不清楚
我回答
咕嚕咕嚕
那個。咕嚕。我的飛機飛過山正朝大海

not that I blamed him
for I saw
at his back a monster on his track
that if he didn't run he'd surely be undone
and I saw
Meimei had a monster at her back
that if she didn't run she'd surely be undone
but there was nothing chasing me but a banana
they had found me under a banana tree you see
so I ran like the wind
I turned on a pin and gobbled it down
I leapt across a babbling brook
saying
leap, Mei, leap!
I saw her take a leap and tumble in quite deep
poor dolly was soaked through and through
I said to her, Mei, don't you want a new mama too?
but *glug glug* was all she said
what's that you say, I can't hear you very clearly
I said in return
but *gulu gulu*
was all she heard
and wouldn't you know! *Putt-putt* went my aeroplane over the
    mountains and far out to sea

You made it like a nursery rhyme! I love it!

Finally, you love something I've done.

I love everything you do, Steve, but some things are more lovable
than others. Funny, but I was thinking about my mom when
you called. You know, after my father died, Ma was quite lost.
She would wander the house aimlessly or just sit in her room for
hours staring at the wall. But then she got dementia and became
very talkative. Much of what she says is nonsense, but it's very
interesting nonsense. I really enjoy our conversations and I think
she does too.

So you got a new mother after all.

I did!

So, are we done now? Can I get back to my life?

Not yet.

What now?

I wrote a draft of "Raised by Wolves" and I want you to translate
it.

You finally wrote the title poem?

Yes! Yes! But I'll need a few days to finish it.

Take all the time in the world, Amang. All the time in the world.

狼養的

三個月爸媽沒有下山
米店不肯再賒帳
我沒力氣爬樹、跑步，祖母牽我
趴到河邊喝個飽

牠來了

很小的時候
我摸著天搖搖晃晃
正在學走的女孩
倒映在牠眼裡被雲包覆，那是我

牠從山上的大岩塊
跳向海邊的礫灘
給礫石帶來火
海水發燙，祖母的床也整晚沸騰
我聽見
他們睡在一起

可惜我終於睡著
直到腳邊堆著暖呼呼
剛被殺死的雞、羊
還有我最愛吃的海魚

祖母又升起爐火，忙碌起來
樹上猴子跳來跳去
一匹野馬衝破了牆，那是我

狼養的

Raised by Wolves

Three months had passed and Ma and Pa had not come down
    the mountain
the local grocery would no longer honor our IOUs
I hadn't the strength to run or climb a tree
Granny led me to the water to drink my fill

then it came

I am very small
I reach for the sky as I wobble back and forth
a child just learning how to stagger
reflected in its eye, embraced by clouds in the sky, that's me

from its mountain lair
It came bounding down to the gravelly shore
setting land and sea on fire
making Granny's bed boil and seethe
I hear them going at it all night long

but then I fall asleep
and wake to find heaped at my feet
freshly slaughtered chicken and sheep
and all the fish I love to eat

Granny is bustling round the fire
a monkey is leaping from tree to tree
a mustang busting through the wall, that's me

Raised by wolves

ACKNOWLEDGMENTS

We wish to thank the editors of the following journals, in which some of the translations first appeared:

Hayden's Ferry Review: "Not Yet"

International Gallerie: "This Poem" and "Papa Was Poor, Mama Bone Dry"

Jacket2: "Love Is Ever So Lovely"

Mānoa: A Pacific Journal of International Writing: "Eating Fish"

Pathlight: "Character Conversion," "Is This Why I Stayed outside the Frame?" and "Raised by Wolves"

Spoon River Poetry Review: "As We Embrace Thousands Are Dying All Over the World," "She Says," "She Said She Couldn't Find Me Last Night and Asked If I'd Been with a Man," and "War Flick"

"Papa Was Poor, Momma Bone Dry" and "As We Embrace Thousands Are Dying All Over the World" were reprinted in *The Art of Women in Contemporary China: Both Sides Now,* ed. Patricia Eichenbaum Karetsky and Zhang Er.

LIST OF ILLUSTRATIONS AND PHOTOGRAPHS

Cover photograph. © Wang Jinren.

Flyleaf photograph. © Amang Hung.

Amang profile photo. © Hua Jin.

Steve Bradbury profile photo. © Clay Holliday.

PARTNERS

pixel |||| texel

ADDITIONAL DONORS, CONT'D

Mark Haber
Mary Cline
Maynard Thomson
Michael Reklis
Mike Soto
Mokhtar Ramadan
Nikki & Dennis Gibson
Patrick Kukucka
Patrick Kutcher
Rev. Elizabeth & Neil Moseley
Richard Meyer

Scott & Katy Nimmons
Sherry Perry
Sydneyann Binion
Stephen Harding
Stephen Williamson
Susan Carp
Susan Ernst
Theater Jones
Tim Perttula
Tony Thomson

SUBSCRIBERS

Audrey Golosky
Ben Nichols
Brittany Johnson
Carol Trimmer
Caroline West
Chana Porter
Charles Dee Mitchell
Charlie Wilcox
Chris Mullikin
Chris Sweet
Courtney Sheedy
Damon Copeland
Derek Maine
Devin McComas
Francisco Fiallo
Fred Griffin
Hillary Richards

Jody Sims
Joe Milazzo
John Winkelman
Lance Stack
Lesley Conzelman
Margaret Terwey
Martha Gifford
Michael Binkley
Michael Elliott
Michael Lighty
Neal Chuang
Radhika
Ryan Todd
Shelby Vincent
Stephanie Barr
William Pate

AVAILABLE NOW FROM DEEP VELLUM

AMANG · *Raised by Wolves*
translated by Steve Bradbury · TAIWAN

MICHÈLE AUDIN · *One Hundred Twenty-One Days*
translated by Christiana Hills · FRANCE

BAE SUAH · *Recitation*
translated by Deborah Smith · SOUTH KOREA

EDUARDO BERTI · *The Imagined Land*
translated by Charlotte Coombe · ARGENTINA

CARMEN BOULLOSA · *Texas: The Great Theft* · *Before* · *Heavens on Earth*
translated by Samantha Schnee · Peter Bush · Shelby Vincent · MEXICO

LEILA S. CHUDORI · *Home*
translated by John H. McGlynn · INDONESIA

SARAH CLEAVE, ed. · *Banthology: Stories from Banned Nations* ·
IRAN, IRAQ, LIBYA, SOMALIA, SUDAN, SYRIA & YEMEN

ANANDA DEVI · *Eve Out of Her Ruins*
translated by Jeffrey Zuckerman · MAURITIUS

ALISA GANIEVA · *Bride and Groom* · *The Mountain and the Wall*
translated by Carol Apollonio · RUSSIA

ANNE GARRÉTA · *Sphinx* · *Not One Day*
translated by Emma Ramadan · FRANCE

JÓN GNARR · *The Indian* · *The Pirate* · *The Outlaw*
translated by Lytton Smith · ICELAND

GOETHE · *The Golden Goblet: Selected Poems*
translated by Zsuzsanna Ozsváth and Frederick Turner · GERMANY

NOEMI JAFFE · *What are the Blind Men Dreaming?*
translated by Julia Sanches & Ellen Elias-Bursac · BRAZIL

CLAUDIA SALAZAR JIMÉNEZ · *Blood of the Dawn*
translated by Elizabeth Bryer · PERU

JUNG YOUNG MOON · *Seven Samurai Swept Away in a River* ·
Vaseline Buddha
translated by Yewon Jung · SOUTH KOREA

KIM YIDEUM · *Blood Sisters*
translated by Ji yoon Lee · SOUTH KOREA

JOSEFINE KLOUGART · *Of Darkness*
translated by Martin Aitken · DENMARK

YANICK LAHENS · *Moonbath*
translated by Emily Gogolak · HAITI

FOUAD LAROUI · *The Curious Case of Dassoukine's Trousers*
translated by Emma Ramadan · MOROCCO

MARIA GABRIELA LLANSOL · *The Geography of Rebels Trilogy: The Book of Communities; The Remaining Life; In the House of July & August*
translated by Audrey Young · PORTUGAL

PABLO MARTÍN SÁNCHEZ · *The Anarchist Who Shared My Name*
translated by Jeff Diteman · SPAIN

DOROTA MASŁOWSKA · *Honey, I Killed the Cats*
translated by Benjamin Paloff · POLAND

BRICE MATTHIEUSSENT · *Revenge of the Translator*
translated by Emma Ramadan · FRANCE

LINA MERUANE · *Seeing Red*
translated by Megan McDowell · CHILE

VALÉRIE MRÉJEN · *Black Forest*
translated by Katie Shireen Assef · FRANCE

FISTON MWANZA MUJILA · *Tram 83*
translated by Roland Glasser · DEMOCRATIC REPUBLIC OF CONGO

GORAN PETROVIĆ · *At the Lucky Hand, aka The Sixty-Nine Drawers*
translated by Peter Agnone · SERBIA

ILJA LEONARD PFEIJFFER · *La Superba*
translated by Michele Hutchison · NETHERLANDS

RICARDO PIGLIA · *Target in the Night*
translated by Sergio Waisman · ARGENTINA

SERGIO PITOL · *The Art of Flight* · *The Journey* ·
The Magician of Vienna · *Mephisto's Waltz: Selected Short Stories*
translated by George Henson · MEXICO

EDUARDO RABASA · *A Zero-Sum Game*
translated by Christina MacSweeney · MEXICO

ZAHIA RAHMANI · *"Muslim": A Novel*
translated by Matthew Reeck · FRANCE/ALGERIA

JUAN RULFO · *The Golden Cockerel & Other Writings*
translated by Douglas J. Weatherford · MEXICO

OLEG SENTSOV · *Life Went On Anyway*
translated by Uilleam Blacker · UKRAINE

MIKHAIL SHISHKIN · *Calligraphy Lesson: The Collected Stories*
translated by Marian Schwartz, Leo Shtutin,
Mariya Bashkatova, Sylvia Maizell · RUSSIA

ÓFEIGUR SIGURÐSSON · *Öræfi: The Wasteland*
translated by Lytton Smith · ICELAND

MUSTAFA STITOU · *Two Half Faces*
translated by David Colmer · NETHERLANDS

FORTHCOMING FROM DEEP VELLUM

MARIO BELLATIN · *Mrs. Murakami's Garden*
translated by Heather Cleary · MEXICO

MAGDA CARNECI · *FEM*
translated by Sean Cotter · ROMANIA

MIRCEA CĂRTĂRESCU · *Solenoid*
translated by Sean Cotter · ROMANIA

MATHILDE CLARK · *Lone Star*
translated by Martin Aitken · DENMARK

LOGEN CURE · *Welcome to Midland: Poems* · USA

PETER DIMOCK · *Daybook from Sheep Meadow* · USA

CLAUDIA ULLOA DONOSO · *Little Bird*, translated by Lily Meyer · PERU/NORWAY

LEYLÂ ERBIL · *A Strange Woman*
translated by Nermin Menemencioğlu · TURKEY

ROSS FARRAR · *Ross Sings Cheree & the Animated Dark: Poems* · USA

FERNANDA GARCIA LAU · *Out of the Cage*
translated by Will Vanderhyden · ARGENTINA

ANNE GARRÉTA · *In/concrete*
translated by Emma Ramadan · FRANCE

GOETHE · *Faust, Part One*
translated by Zsuzsanna Ozsváth and Frederick Turner · GERMANY

JUNG YOUNG MOON · *Arriving in a Thick Fog*
translated by Mah Eunji and Jeffrey Karvonen · SOUTH KOREA

DMITRY LIPSKEROV · *The Tool and the Butterflies*
translated by Reilly Costigan-Humes & Isaac Stackhouse Wheeler · RUSSIA

FISTON MWANZA MUJILA · *The Villain's Dance*, translated by Roland Glasser · *The River in the Belly: Selected Poems*, translated by Bret Maney · DEMOCRATIC REPUBLIC OF CONGO

LUDMILLA PETRUSHEVSKAYA · *Kidnapped: A Crime Story*, translated by Marian Schwartz · *The New Adventures of Helen: Magical Tales*, translated by Jane Bugaeva · RUSSIA

JULIE POOLE · *Bright Specimen: Poems from the Texas Herbarium* · USA

MANON STEFAN ROS · *The Blue Book of Nebo* · WALES

ETHAN RUTHERFORD · *Farthest South & Other Stories* · USA

BOB TRAMMELL · *The Origins of the Avant-Garde in Dallas & Other Stories* · USA